THE
AMBITIOUS
WOMAN'S
GUIDE
to
a
SUCCESSFUL
CAREER

THE AMBITIOUS WOMAN'S GUIDE to a SUCCESSFUL CAREER

MARGARET V. HIGGINSON
and
THOMAS L. QUICK

A DIVISION OF AMERICAN MANAGEMENT ASSOCIATIONS

to Pam and Lisa

Library of Congress Cataloging in Publication Data

Higginson, M   Valliant.
  The ambitious woman's guide to a successful career.

  Bibliography: p.
  1. Women executives. 2. Women in business.
3. Success. I. Quick, Thomas L., joint author.
II. Title.
HF5500.2.H49   331.4'81'6584   75-6870
ISBN 0-8144-5378-3

Fourth Printing

PREFACE

IF you are a woman planning to embark on a career—whether you are entering a business organization for the first time, resuming work after an interruption, or already working and looking for a way upward —this book is intended for you. Even if your motivation is uncertain and the level of your aspirations not very high, we hope it encourages you to make a firm commitment to goals that will ultimately lead to a successful career.

The suggestions and guidelines offered reflect the realities of organizational life today, realities that you must consider in defining and recognizing your career goals. We hope the book will help you to evaluate what obstacles you might have to overcome to achieve equality with men in the business world; to consider what opportunities you can reasonably anticipate; and to recognize and develop the resources upon which you can draw.

Admittedly, any book written on women's careers at this time is an incomplete statement. Fast-changing conditions make it impossible for a publication to remain definitive for any length of time. Each day sees new developments emerging through legislation, litigation, publicity, and pressures exerted by women's groups. New career paths are being blazed in our increasingly service-oriented economy, and doors to managerial positions that were once labeled ''for men only'' are now open.

We recognize that there are no universal formulas for getting ahead, but there are methods that can assist in the shaping of your own career objectives and strategies. This book is a plain-speaking guide to those methods. *You*—your unique mix of abilities, aptitudes, interests, and life style—will be the chief determinant of the success you achieve. Consequently we strongly emphasize the need for continuing assessment of yourself, development of the largest number of choices, and improvement of your skills.

If this book does nothing else for you, let it convey a sense of urgency: You have no time to waste in planning your career. True, conditions are getting better in this country for women who want business careers. True, there is and will be more acceptance of women in business, more jobs and career paths open to them, more education and training available as time passes. But you might as well be realistic; *whenever* you start climbing, you will still encounter the same obstacles women have been encountering for years. In many organizations, men and women start at the same approximate level but more men are put on the fast track that leads to greater responsibility, higher salary increases, and earlier and more frequent promotions. As a woman, you will have to start as early as possible—and work harder and smarter than most men who are your peers.

Another reason why you should not delay your career planning is our uncertain economy. Most business organizations have trimmed their fat: There are fewer responsible jobs than there were a few years ago, and more people—some very experienced—competing for those positions. The competition will become even more fierce in the next decade, as the shortage of middle management personnel eases. Because of the low birth rates of the 1930s and early 1940s, business organizations have had relatively few people in the 35-to-55-year range to promote. But now the first crop of the post–World War II baby boom is reaching age 30.

There's still another reason why women should strive to move upward now. The federal government has become tougher about enforcing compliance with equal-rights and equal-pay laws and regulations. Business organizations, large and small, are actively seeking women to place in positions that have been traditionally occupied by men. No matter how much a corporation cuts its recruiting efforts, it will still probably specify that a certain number of women will be seriously considered for the available positions.

Finally, the plain fact is that the longer you wait, the greater is the probability that you will be competing not only with men but with growing numbers of other qualified women. Slowly but surely, ambitious career-minded women are beginning to break into the professions and occupations that are traditionally male, such as finance, engineering, and marketing. The competition is keen.

It is unusual for the authors of a book to state that they hope their book will rapidly become outdated, but we hope ours will. While times and conditions are changing fast, all signs indicate that it will take many years to overcome the decades of conditioning, to overcome the biases that keep doors from opening wide. Equality is a goal, not an actuality. Therefore, you might as well brace yourself for the fact that you'll have to cope with traditional attitudes, feelings, and responses—both in yourself and in others—for many years to come. And if you want to be upwardly mobile, you'll probably have to be more aggressive, alert, shrewd, and determined than your male counterparts. It is our hope that this book will help you develop those traits—or discover them in yourself.

THE AUTHORS

CONTENTS

1

THE
MORE
THINGS
CHANGE...

RECENTLY a young woman we know, armed with a newly acquired higher degree in the behavioral sciences, went looking for a job. One of her interviews was with a consulting firm. Her discussion with a partner in the firm was pleasant and relaxed; in fact, it went on for most of the afternoon without specific reference to the position to be filled. Finally, out of frustration, the woman asked the partner to describe the job he had in mind.

There was no opening, he told her. Taken aback, she asked him why he had responded to her résumé. The rest of the exchange went like this:

"Some of the partners think it's time we had a woman in the firm."

"How do *you* feel about hiring a woman?" she asked.

"Well, my own feeling is that we have enough problems already. But maybe they're right," he answered.

Trying to conceal her anger, she asked him, "What happens now?"

"I was thinking about talking to an acquaintance of mine in Chicago. His firm hired a woman a few months ago, and I'd like to ask him how she worked out."

When this young woman tells the story of her interview, she very often gets laughter—from men. Some men can't conceive of such stupidity or insensitivity or rudeness—or all three. But there are many women who can empathize with this job hunter's experience in humiliation (only one of several, she reports, in her search for a job). They know there is often a vast difference between the way a woman is interviewed and considered for a responsible position and the treatment a man receives.

Equality of opportunity and pay for women is the law. There are harsh penalties for denying this equality, as AT&T, Northwest Airlines, and others are learning. In 1973, a survey [1] of 111 organizations by *Industrial Relations News* and *Recruiting Trends,* two weekly newsletters, revealed that almost 80 percent of those organizations were feeling pressure to provide more opportunities for female employees, and that that pressure was coming from government agencies such as the Equal Employment Opportunity Commission and the Office of Federal Contract Compliance of the Department of Labor. "EEOC's docket of complaints keeps growing," the survey reports, "indicating increasing willingness on the part of women to press a case." [2]

Women's groups such as the National Organization for Women (NOW) have become potent forces. There are employment agencies; search firms that specialize in placing women (one, Catalyst, has a nationwide computerized system to match women and jobs); women's counseling services; women's political, social, and professional groups; women's publications, such as periodicals and directories; and most of these are developments of the last few years to help women find careers.

Three-quarters of the organizations contacted by *Industrial Relations News* and *Recruiting Trends* said they had women employees in jobs formerly held by men. In a recent speech, Lena B.

Prewitt, of the University of Alabama at Tuscaloosa, described what is happening to women on the work scene as "a revolution in the *type* of work performed by women, in the *place* of work for women, and in the *conditions* of her work. Women have made inroads into all types of occupations and have assumed roles ranging from long-distance truck drivers to corporate presidents and from bartenders to professional football players." [3]

The educational level of these younger women who are making inroads is rising. A report of the U.S. Department of Commerce observed that "the increases in educational level for younger women have been great—18 percent of women 20 to 24 years old had completed some college in 1957, compared with 32 percent in 1967, and 34 percent in 1972." [4]

More than 3,000 women showed up in Chicago in March 1974 to form the Coalition of Labor Union Women, among whose objectives are "to encourage unions to organize unorganized women . . . to encourage women to fight job discrimination . . . to push child care legislation [and] passage of the ERA [Equal Rights Amendment]."

It would seem that women do have more opportunities for employment than they did previously. They have the full force of federal authority behind them. The once suspect and scorned feminist groups have achieved acceptance. Top management in all sorts of organizations is broadcasting a commitment to provide opportunities for qualified women. The number of educated, ambitious, career-minded women increases each year. Universities and other management education facilities, such as the American Management Associations, are offering a growing number of seminars and courses to help women in their career progress. Even unions are feeling the pressure from women to create more job opportunities for females.

Furthermore, when you consider that, because of the extraordinarily low birth rate of the 1930s, there is a shortage of males between 35 and 45 to fill management positions in organizations, and when you also consider that the cutback in management training and development during the recession of the early 1970s has rendered that shortage of qualified men more acute, you must surely conclude that these are truly auspicious times for women who want careers and responsible, challenging work.

A CLOSER LOOK

However, few women feel that there is much to cheer about just yet. C. F. Fretz and Joanne Hayman share this less than optimistic view:

> Despite the government's dicta, and despite the passion, rhetoric, and emotion supporting EEO for women, persuading many businesses to judge female managerial candidates in the same light as they do males is far from accomplished. . . . Just as women must exhibit a readiness to accept the added responsibilities associated with EEO, so companies must want, not just be willing, to provide opportunities for females who are sincerely interested in pursuing business careers. Yet until business is economically threatened by the consumer, as well as by the government, it is unlikely that EEO progress for women will be other than slow.[5]

"By and large," concludes *The Wall Street Journal,* "women aren't getting many important corporate posts. Their advancement stops short of the executive suite, their authority ends short of final decision-making power." [6] Essentially the same judgment can be made about women's progress (that is, their lack of it) in government and service institutions.

Common Obstacles to Upward Mobility

There are a number of discernible reasons why ambitious, career-minded women are finding it difficult to make upward progress in organizations.

Fuzzy promotion criteria. The Peter Principle—in a hierarchy a person tends to rise to his or her level of incompetence—is regarded as a funny explanation of the presence of so many incompetent people in organizations. But this principle contains an essential truth. One reason why so many people *do* rise above their competence is that the measuring and evaluation techniques employed in most organizations are so unreliable that there is no sure way of knowing how far a person is capable of going until he or she has demonstrated by incompetence that too much advancement has been made.

In addition, the promotion criteria themselves have not been codified in most organizations. Carmen R. Maymi, director of the Women's Bureau of the U.S. Department of Labor, relates the case of a high-level executive addressing a group of women. His message to them was that he would be only too happy to promote qualified women, but the unfortunate fact was that there weren't many around. One of the women asked him to describe the qualifications that accounted for *his* rise in the hierarchy. After much fumbling, backing and filling, he sat down without really answering the question.[7] Obviously a woman will find it difficult to prove that she is qualified for a position if no one is quite sure of what the proper qualifications are. And that is what many women are finding.

Bare compliance. For many male managers, "this whole EEO business" is just one more government constraint on private enterprise. Thus, the interest is in complying with the requirements and not much more. Some organizations have already achieved some publicity for their elaborate and progressive affirmative action plans (*plans!*). But there may have been no real implementation of those plans. In many organizations the EEO officer or coordinator is a man without much understanding of—perhaps without sympathy for—the disadvantaged females in the lower echelons of the hierarchy.

Managers whose concern is mere compliance in order to avoid penalty will find any number of tactics to conceal discriminatory practice. For example, they'll go through the motions of interviewing women when they have already selected a man for the position. Moreover, even though higher-echelon or staff managers manifest a sincere interest in developing women as resources, many line and lower-echelon managers and supervisors do not understand what is involved. If managers don't understand the need or the sanctions, they won't be willing participants in an affirmative action program.

Inadequate education. Feminist counselors as well as recruiters point out that many women who come out of universities and colleges with liberal arts degrees expect to find responsible jobs open to them. These women are ignoring the realities that successful young men have been aware of for several decades: The best jobs and starting salaries—and, for the most part, career paths—go to the applicants with a specialized background and a technical degree. At present, a woman who has an accounting or engineering degree is much in demand; and if in addition she has a master's degree in business administration, she is well armed for competition with male applicants.

Undetected capability. To a great extent, women in organizations have not been considered for management or professional training and development. The EEO administrator in one large corporation wondered why no women had gone through the corporate assessment center that had been established two years before. She learned that no employees whose positions were below a certain grade were being considered for assessment—and the positions of almost all the women employed by the firm were below that grade. She persuaded corporate management to lower the requirements so that women could be included in the assessment program.

Other organizations have refused to consider women for advanced training because they feel women are less likely to remain in the career paths than men are. Likelihood of pregnancy, lack of commitment, reluctance to relocate—all have been used as justifications for excluding women from training.

There is little question that if you decide *not* to look for talent in a certain area, you are likely not to find it there.

Backlash. Some male employees of Bell System companies have suggested that any man who wants a promotion in the system (which has been hard hit by financial penalties resulting from adverse judgments in discrimination suits) had better submit to a sexchange operation. And some women who consider that they have made it in a man's world without help (especially from militant women's groups) are likely to say that other women today have it easier than they should.

Clearly, the pressures being exerted on organizations by women—and by the government on behalf of women—produce negative reactions in some men and women. And in some cases these negative responses are translated into subversion and sabotage of the efforts of women and organizations to provide more upward mobility paths for women.

It is interesting that women managers often report that some of the most pronounced resistance to their advancement comes from other women who seem to have no similar ambitions, or from women who display the traditional prejudice against working for a woman (presumably, working for a woman carries less status than working for a man). At least part of the resistance shown by women to the success of other women may derive from their resentment over destruction of the rationalization that women cannot succeed because they are women. When some women do get ahead, a new rationalization for individual lack of effort has to be found.

Prevailing myths. It is hard for men to accept the fact that women who work need to work. According to the U.S. Department of Labor, 40 percent of all working women are not financially dependent on either a husband or a father. And a significant percentage of married women work in order to keep their family above the poverty level.

But in talking of career planning, of mobility into professional and managerial positions, we are obviously not talking about the survival aspects of earning wages. We do not question a woman's need to sustain herself—and her family. However, there is a difference between a *job,* which pays the bills, and a *career,* which can provide a person with a sense of fulfillment. The importance of self-fulfillment in one's work has not been given its rightful place by many of us. We are still being influenced by the Protestant ethic and the subsistence value—the external rewards—of work. We have only recently begun to evaluate work in terms of its internal rewards—personal satisfaction, self-actualization, expertness, self-esteem, and so forth.

Inordinate pressure. There are bound to be failures, and some people will certainly say, "Well, you see, women just aren't suitable (or ready) for this sort of thing." Some women will be promoted to positions they shouldn't occupy—at least not without extensive training and experience, which, in many cases, they won't get. Others will find that they are the token or pilot woman, and the pressure to succeed for the benefit of womankind will be unendurable. In addition to the challenges of any new and responsible position, the woman is likely to encounter the unwillingness of certain male and female employees (both peers and superiors) to work with her because she is a woman. And, in a job never before held by a woman, she could hardly be blamed for feeling a bit paranoid; she is probably right that some of those around her would not only be happy if she fell on her face but might even set up roadblocks to increase the chances of her failure.

A man's world—still. The structure of many, perhaps most, organizations favors men. Usually the lower-level jobs traditionally held by women are dead ends—there are no upward channels from them. Most organizations are geared to full-time employment, one person per job, with nearly everyone working the same hours. The exclusion of part-time employment, floating hours and flexible scheduling, job sharing (two employees perform the same job at different times), and split locations (an employee works part of the time in an office and part of the time at home) severely limits the contributions that many women can make.

However bright the promise of the cultural, economic, and social changes now taking place, the stark and discouraging fact remains that the woman who seeks a career in organizations still dominated by men and who is determined to enjoy equality of opportunity and esteem will in most cases be confronted by obstacles that men with similar ambitions do not face. These obstacles are placed in her path primarily because she is a woman seeking admittance to and membership in a man's world. And in many cases, she may have placed some of those obstacles in her path herself.

THE CONVENTIONAL MALE AND FEMALE ATTITUDES

"Two major barriers . . . must still be broken before women workers will gain equity," wrote Susan Ells, describing the affirmative action program at Polaroid Corporation, where she is EEO coordinator. "The first barrier . . . is male managers' stereotypes of what a female worker should or should not do; the second barrier is the woman herself. Lacking models in management or in skilled trade jobs, women are not yet convinced that secretarial and teaching positions are not the only available or appropriate options." [8]

What Ells has observed on the Polaroid scene can be applied generally. The attitudes that men have toward women, that women have toward men, and that each sex has about itself can enhance the success of the revolution—but instead they seem to be providing the counterrevolution in most organizations.

We are not aware of the formation of these attitudes in ourselves. We don't know the extent of their influence on us. Many of these attitudes are assumed to be based on logic and fact. They often go unchallenged, and when they are challenged, the rebuttal is misdirected and ineffective. Because these attitudes are ingrained, taken for granted, obstructive, and hard to detect, both men and women in organizations need to bring them to the surface, to define them—and to deal with them.

In 1972, consultants Billie Alban and Gail Silverman conducted a workshop for men and women of the National Organization Development Network. The data produced in the workshop showed how deep and extensive is the conditioning that both sexes have received. The network is a professional association of people engaged in personnel activities, training, and consulting in government, business, and nonprofit institutions. Many of them have degrees in the behavioral sciences. All ages are represented. Their political and social orientations tend to be liberal.

The purpose of the workshop, entitled "Men's Role in Women's Equality," was to help both men and women to examine their feelings about the equality of the sexes. In order to generate data about these feelings, all-male groups listed the advantages and disadvantages of promoting women, and all-female groups listed the advantages and disadvantages of being promoted, to positions of power and influence.

The advantages listed by the male groups included some rather predictable responses, for example, "satisfies government requirements," "improve utilization of untapped human resources," "pleasure of working with women on an equal basis," "increases potential of having women as friends," "encourages other women to follow suit and seek advancement."

But other statements of the advantages of promoting women into positions of leadership were not so automatic and clear-cut: "diversity is stimulating," "women are better managers than men," "stimulating to take risks, and moving women into positions of profit and loss is a risk," "women bring a new dimension [affective] to problem-solving," "seduction would become an option for upward influencing."

These statements seem to say that women are different and that their behavior and skills will be different. Some of them suggest that it will be quite a novelty having women around, or that having women as managers will be therapeutic or corrective for men: for example, "free me up from responsibilities and guilt," "personal growth for me," "more fun," "I want women to like me," "bring more personal liberation to men," "I think women are good allies; they do things I can't do."

Keep in mind that these comments were made by men who believed they were presenting arguments in favor of promoting women into positions of responsibility. Yet they show little awareness of what women in such positions could contribute to the organizational welfare. With a few exceptions, most of the responses suggest the impact on either the person making the comment or on the men in the organization who would be working closely with women.

Here are sample statements, as reported by Alban and Silverman, reflecting the male groups' views of the potential *disadvantages* of moving women into positions of power and influence:

Loss of domination implicit in being a "gentleman."
Male roles will need to change, with resulting uncertainty and conflicts.
Conflicts arising out of husband-wife competitiveness.
Harder to work with.
Threat to male self-image.
Makes working out sexual hang-ups more difficult.
Requires a new interpersonal style.
Destroys romantic image.
Introduces emotions into logical management decisions.
Women don't like to work with other women.
Men don't like to work with women.

Difficult to separate personal and professional roles.

Women might tend to be biased and promote women only.

If married, women might not invest sufficient time and energy in home role.

Increased competition in job market.

New demands on male/father/husband roles.

Differing Perceptions, Double Standards

Psychologist Jane W. Torrey writes that a woman "is supposed to be *submissive, passive,* and *dependent* in contrast to men who are *assertive, independently responsible,* and *full of initiative.* Women are reputed to be *diligent,* especially at *routines,* rather than *imaginative* like men. They are *selfless* and *devoted,* rather than *ambitious* like men." (Emphasis hers.)

Pursuing the difference in perceptions of men and women, Torrey also writes, "A woman who works hard is content with dull, repetitive work; a diligent man is working his way to the top. A woman who accepts reproof is submissive; a man who does the same is 'biding his time.' A woman who is upset by reproof is being emotional; a man who does the same is refusing to be pushed around." [9]

Volumes could be written about the many ways in which men discriminate against women. In organizations, some forms of this discriminatory behavior are merely annoying—"You really think like a man!"—while others are quite malicious and destructive. According to Margaret Hennig, associate professor at Simmons College, a male manager may go to extreme lengths to protect himself against the entry of women. He may deliberately hire less competent women so that when they fail, he can say, "I told you it wouldn't work." Or he may resort to overt hostility and overt action to destroy a competent woman. [10]

Eleanor Brantley Schwartz and James J. Rago, Jr. expand this theme:

> He attempts to ruin the effectiveness of the woman through conscious or unconscious sabotage. He may use her as a scapegoat for errors he has made. . . . He seeks to avoid the situation by isolating his department as much as possible from the influence of the

woman. . . . He withholds help and information she needs to learn her job.[11]

Women are accustomed to being singled out: "It's nice to see so many of the ladies here." They are constantly reminded that they are not regular, equal members of the group—"Let's hear from the ladies first." When a man uses an off-color word, there are instant apologies for the disrespect shown women. On the less "polite" side, a female vice president, the only woman in her firm's executive suite, was publicly chastised by the president during an evening executive session for not having set the table for the dinner that had been brought in.

Women have experienced other kinds of reminders that they should not assume they are men's equals. One woman waited 20 years to gain her first management position. And she gained it largely by forcing the issue—she would not accept anything less. She knew that a new department was about to be created, similar to two departments already in existence. Yet, when the department was formed, and she was installed as its head, she was told to report not to the vice president, as the other two managers did, but to those two department heads.

Another woman who was promoted to supervisor was angered by the way the promotion was made. "A man would have been called in," she claimed, "and asked whether he wanted the job. I was told I had the job, because, of course, my boss figured he knew exactly how my mind worked." When promoted to a job previously held by a man, other women have found that the job has been narrowed in responsibility or that its title has been changed.

Here are some frequent and annoying manifestations of male discriminatory behavior. He:

- assumes that any woman answering the phone is a secretary, or that any woman sitting in a room full of men must be someone's secretary recruited to take notes.
- not only refers to his secretary as a "girl," he assumes ownership: she is "my girl."
- makes a production of helping women co-workers on with their coats, opening doors for them, lighting their cigarettes.

- suggests to males when a female is present that he has some good jokes to tell when the woman leaves; or ostentatiously launders a joke so he can tell it before the woman.
- sets up luncheons in private clubs that will not accept women as members or even permit them equal access to the club (one famous club requires all female guests to ride up in the service elevator to reach the dining room).
- pats women on the head when he is pleased with them and says things like, "You're a real doll."
- feels compelled to flirt if there is a woman in the group and to let everyone know how sexually attracted to her he is (even if he isn't). And she is supposed to regard this as a compliment.
- rephrases what a woman has just said, as if her comments are deficient, not understandable, or not acceptable to others the way she expressed them.

Men have been conditioned to look down on women, to regard the feminine sex as weaker, less logical, less aggressive, and less creative for so long—centuries, in fact—that it is amazing that people have begun to seriously and successfully question the basis of that conditioning. And, as we shall see, the conditioning has been successful with women, too. The conviction that women are inferior is so subtle and ingrained in men that they often aren't aware of it. Many a male will deny he is a chauvinist, then tell or laugh at a joke that degrades women. He will consider himself so innocent of any behavior that discriminates against women that he can stand up, as one young man did in an open forum we attended, and ask impatiently, "What is it you women want? Tell me, so I know what to give you." We know of a man who, having once worked for a woman, attested sincerely to his belief that women should not be discriminated against because of their sex; yet, a few days later he said he'd never work for a woman boss again.

Women's Attitudes That Stand in Their Way

At a recent conference of executive secretaries and administrative assistants, the subject of male prejudice came up. After listening to several accounts of women who had been discriminated against by male bosses and co-workers, one secretary spoke up: "I've been shocked to see how women discriminate against themselves.'' She then explained that at a previous job she had taken over her boss's duty of composing letters, but she had continued to sign his name; it never occurred to her to identify herself and her work.

Another woman talked about being sent to an out-of-town meeting of executives that her boss was unable to attend. Self-conscious about being the only woman in the conference room, she took a seat in the corner instead of at the table. She did not consider herself a full-fledged member of the group, even though she was there as a proxy for her boss. She told herself she would listen carefully and take information about what went on back to her boss.

It isn't only male attitudes and biases that constitute obstructions for the upwardly mobile woman. Forces within the woman herself, and within other women, pose threats to her success. Here are some of the disadvantages of being promoted to positions of power and influence given by the women at the workshop held by Alban and Silverman:

> Managing husband's feelings.
> Demands on time, conflict with home responsibilities.
> Danger of becoming overassertive or of being perceived as unfeminine.
> Desire to stay in the woman's traditional role without feeling guilty.
> Fear and anxiety because our society doesn't condition women to think of themselves as power figures.

Other statements suggested conflict arising from the change in relationships with friends, family, and co-workers. In their comments the women also expressed suspicions and resentments about the burdens that would be placed on them because they were women:

> Protecting and tending the fragile male ego.
> Buying masculine values.
> Feelings of representing the whole female sex.
> Not knowing whether I am chosen for my sex or my competence.
> Being left out of the ''men's room'' decision-making process.

These women feel that they will not be looked at by men as individuals but as representatives of *women* in general, and that in reality they won't have much power (and what power they do have will be only as much as men will give them).

Women wonder if success will arouse hostility in their co-workers, both male and female, if it will make them social outcasts in the office, or among their friends; if it will upset their husbands. "Women are taught not to compete—and if they compete, not to win. . . . The lesson is, you won't be popular if you win." [12] And many women fear that this is true.

The Queen Bee Syndrome

According to one woman experienced in counseling and placing women in responsible government and business positions, many women who have reached management levels seem no more interested than men in seeing that female resources are developed and utilized more fully. And some women who have become successful are classified as antifeminists. Graham Staines, Carol Tavris, and Toby Epstein Jararatne describe this antifeminism as the Queen Bee syndrome. "Many successful women . . . relish the fact that they are 'special,' that they have unique qualifications that allow them to get high-ranking positions normally denied to women. Non-discriminatory policies become threatening. Queen Bees do not want competition for their jobs any more than the men do." Usually, the Queen Bee has had a hard climb up. Why, she asks, should other women have it easier? Besides, she feels more identity with the male colleagues who have accepted her than with women as a class. "The irony of it all is that the Queen Bee, because of her access to power and male favor, is in the best position to advance the cause of women, but is the least inclined to do so." [13]

STANDING TALLER, NOT REDUCING OTHERS

Men and women have adopted prejudices against each other for the simple reason that such prejudices can be self-serving. They save wear and tear on the brain. When you automatically resort to stereotypes, you don't have to think. Prejudices are protective; they keep you from worrying about whether or not you are superior. And they justify discriminatory behavior.

But in the long run, and in the short run as well, prejudicial behavior is both self-destructive and destructive of others. In most cases, successful people in organizations enhance their career progress by effectively utilizing the available resources (and resources are not graded by sex). In addition, people who really climb far up the ladder tend to discover that the way to achieve is by developing their own talents, not by reducing the stature of those around them.

REFERENCES

1. *What's Ahead in Personnel.* A supplement to *Industrial Relations News* (published by Industrial Relations News, Chicago, March 1973).
2. Ibid., pp. 1–2.
3. Lena B. Prewitt, "The Employment Rights of the Female." Speech delivered at the Personnel Meeting of the Southeastern Electric Exchange, Baton Rouge, La., October 4, 1973.
4. "Occupation, Employment, and Lifetime Work Experience of Women." Papers prepared by Larry E. Suter. (Washington, D.C.: U.S. Department of Commerce, Social and Economic Statistics Administration, Bureau of the Census, August 1973), p. 5.
5. C. F. Fretz and Joanne Hayman, "Progress for Women—Men Are Still More Equal," *Harvard Business Review,* September–October 1973.
6. "Despite Much Hoopla, Few Women Capture Companies' Top Jobs," *The Wall Street Journal,* April 18, 1974.
7. Personal interview, November 1973.
8. Susan C. Ells, "How Polaroid Gave Women the Kind of Affirmative Action Program They Wanted," *Management Review,* November 1973, p. 14.
9. Jane W. Torrey, "A Psychologist's Look at Women," *Journal of Contemporary Business,* Summer 1973, p. 26.
10. Margaret Hennig, "Women in Management: What Needs to Be Done?" Dupont *Context,* Vol. 1, 1974, pp. 13–16.
11. Eleanor Brantley Schwartz and James J. Rago, Jr., "Beyond Tokenism: Women as True Corporate Peers," *Business Horizons,* December 1973, pp. 69–76.
12. *Woman Power,* February 1974, p. 7.
13. Graham Staines, Carol Tavris, Toby Epstein Jararatne, "The Queen Bee Syndrome," *Psychology Today,* January 1974, pp. 55–60.

2

SUCCESS DETERMINANTS AND DETERRENTS

WHAT do you want to be when you grow up?'' is a familiar question that adults ask small children, even before they are in school. And children respond with whatever occupation has recently captured their imagination. A boy says he wants to be a cowboy, a pilot, or another traditional American male hero; a girl says she'd like to be a nurse, a teacher, or a mother, traditional female roles. And adults nod approval.

Children's lives are full of transactions like this that mean little to the adults involved. But they may mean a great deal to the youngsters. Such transactions can condition and reinforce the children's thinking, shape their attitudes and beliefs, and to an extent predetermine their future behavior and activities. Although a certain amount of reinforcing and shaping occurs throughout our lives, many of our responses and feelings are already established before we reach adulthood. Only by making a conscious effort to modify our patterns and psychological sets, to break the molds forced on us as children, can we overcome the effects of our conditioning and the invisible internal barriers that so often inhibit our freedom of progress.

THE CONDITIONING PROCESS

Women in our society have their own mental and emotional set, which, like that of men, is culturally determined by their families, teachers, older friends, and other adults who serve as models. Though the way men and women view themselves and relate to others is established in childhood and reinforced during adolescence, the reinforcement of most women continues into adult life.

During childhood, girls receive what Cynthia Epstein refers to as "docility training." This pleases their fathers who want them to be "feminine," and it also helps them do well in school because they learn to follow instructions and carry out assignments.[1] Good grades and good behavior win approval from teachers, as well as from parents.

Girls are taught to socialize, sympathize, and empathize, especially if they have brothers and sisters, and they are encouraged to learn household arts—sewing and needlework, cooking and meal preparation, child care, and so on. They are discouraged from building bookshelves, participating in athletic or outdoor activities, and excelling in sports. Boys are sent to camps and special schools more often than girls, since these represent an investment in the boys' future. Girls get piano lessons, dancing classes, and secretarial courses to teach them skills and activities that will enhance them socially. At this point girls are also learning to dress and adorn themselves in preparation for dating, and ultimately marriage, while the boys are pitting their strength (physical and psychological) against that of other boys and learning to compete in preparation for their adult pursuits—careers, club memberships, and other "male" activities.

In later years this conditioning is reinforced. The girl or young woman who behaves aggressively, preferring physical sports and hobbies, and choosing a career instead of marriage, receives all kinds of signals of disapproval from friends and acquaintances, and sometimes she even encounters open hostility. Her female friends feel sorry for her because she has no husband or children. Because she has chosen a career, she is excluded from many of her friends' in-group activities, just as she is from those of male friends.

But many women never reach the career stage. They become housewives (they may have jobs) primarily because they don't outgrow the lessons painstakingly taught them. Since they cannot overcome the conditioning received in their early years, they become what their parents wanted them to become and exhibit these characteristics:

Passivity: Instead of being action-oriented, these women sit back and wait for another person (usually a man) to initiate action, to make decisions about what needs to be done and about when and how transactions should take place.

Dependency: They are not self-sufficient, not able to stand on their own feet and "go it alone." Instead of desiring freedom, the thought of it makes them uncomfortable; they want and need to be supported financially and emotionally, which often results in the husband's taking over the role of father.

Diffidence: As a result of years of deferring and taking a back seat to men, these women lack self-confidence and self-reliance. They are easily intimidated by persons who profess to have more experience, knowledge, and skills (usually men).

Submissiveness: This trait is characterized by an absence of leadership qualities. The women tend to be followers, to take orders better than they give them (many people believe this trait to be inherent in women).

Docility: These females are easily managed and taught. This characteristic is typically found in young girls and women who are eager to please their elders—primarily their fathers, and later their husbands; secondarily, their mothers and female teachers.

Inferiority: Low self-esteem in these women causes them to think of themselves as second-class citizens who are not valued highly by society. Some women, especially those whose husbands believe they are superior at everything, feel totally worthless.

Noncompetitiveness: These women dislike participating in activities in which physical or mental efforts are pitted or measured against each other and one will either win or lose (this is attributed to women's low level of aggressiveness). They especially dislike visible games and contests.

Methods of Coping

Women handle these feelings and characteristics in a variety of ways. They deny them and pretend they don't exist; they minimize their importance; they explain them away. Some women laugh and shrug them off, but most don't—for example, the woman who gets tears in her eyes when her husband or boss talks down to her in front of other people. Women's liberationists, who are fighting these behavioral characteristics, frequently bristle and resist when someone tries to force them into a submissive role. Some women use feminine behavior patterns to get what they want. Estelle Ramey, professor of physiology and biochemistry at Georgetown University, compares a woman's situation with that of a young boy of 16 or 17 who is dependent, powerless, and has to ask for money and permission to use the car. "In order to get what she wants," says Dr. Ramey, "a woman learns to wheedle, to pout, to manipulate, to be essentially an outsized child. And it works very well, unless what she wants is to grow up." [2]

The way women handle their feelings about how they are treated can be as much a problem as the feelings themselves. After years of sublimating, repressing, and rationalizing, many women find it difficult to express themselves openly, to admit their anxieties and fears, and to level about their feelings when they really need to. In fact, even when they try to be open, they often hesitate to speak out because they are so used to having their feelings and opinions trampled on. They realize that open discussion and confrontation can result in their being and feeling more disadvantaged than they did previously.

According to Jane Torrey,[3] a psychologist at Connecticut College, reluctance to perceive oneself as victim is a real psychological barrier for women. She states:

> People like to think they have done as well as possible in life: no-
> body enjoys being told that she might have been happier, richer or

more successful if it weren't for some injustice. . . . The woman who toils daily at dull and ill-paid or unpaid work and who sees no means of changing it has a strong motive to think that it is inevitable or only fair or even virtuous. A stupid boss is a joke as long as you do not contemplate how much better you could have done his job, but, if you had dared to aspire to his position and salary yourself, he would be salt in the wound.

These conditions don't apply to all women, and the world is changing. But we still haven't moved very far from Philip Wylie's Cinderella story, popular a generation ago. There are thousands of women who are passive or active dependents—and this condition is not affected by whether they work or stay home all day, are married or single or divorced, have children, belong to a women's group, go to school, or are making an effort to think, feel, or be independent. And there are still thousands of men who are incapable, unwilling, or reluctant to concede that women should have the same privileges, rights, and freedom that they themselves have.

Roles and Relationships

Several years ago Margaret Hennig studied a small number of top-level women executives (presidents and vice presidents) and found a remarkable similarity in their backgrounds. Every one of them was either an only child or the firstborn in a family with all daughters and had an exceptionally close relationship with her father. Not only did she have a close attachment to her father and his career, but he in effect served as her manager. As a child, she was never conditioned to accept a traditional role, and she was allowed to participate in boys' activities, such as baseball, if she wished. When she grew up, she was allowed to enter a man's field. Each woman had a tremendous sense of self-esteem.[4]

Once these women entered the business world, each one followed this pattern:

- She "hooked up" with a male manager several levels above her, moved up the organization ladder with him, and benefited from his breaking down organizational barriers for her.
- She conceived of herself as a technical specialist and concentrated on becoming an expert in her technical area.

- She doggedly stuck with the company, considered it her family, but related strongly to no one and became rigid, hard, cold, and uncommunicative.
- She found some way to resolve her identity crisis as a woman during her middle 30s, middle management years by integrating her executive role with her role as a woman. One of the women had herself revamped at Elizabeth Arden.
- Half of the women married older men who were super-achievers and either widowers or divorcés with children.
- None of the women had children of her own.
- The marriages were considered happy, but in some cases the couple devoted so much time to their careers that they had only one day a week together.[5]

Sandra Brown points out that successful women executives usually have at least one parent or a close relative who is an aggressive, positive-minded leader.[6]

In talking with women in their 20s who have high aspirations and those in their 30s who have proven themselves to be high achievers, we found that a number of them were either the oldest child or the only child in a family headed by a father who is either an entrepreneur, business executive, or professional, with whom they strongly identified. In a few cases, the mother's influence was as strong or stronger, either because she herself had a career or because she wished that she had one.

Although there is no conclusive evidence to support the theory that firstborn and only children (male and female) are the most successful, some studies do indicate that they are high performers. Two reasons for this are that as children many of them receive more parental attention and discipline and that if they have brothers and sisters, they assume a responsible role in the family.

In the traditional family, the oldest son eventually takes over the father's role as head of the family and of the family business, if there is one. In the contemporary family, the oldest daughter in an all-girl family, or in a family in which the brothers are considerably younger, may, as a "substitute" oldest son, go to college and have a career. Of course, many parents encourage daughters to attend college, but few urge them to become doctors, lawyers, engineers, architects, or college professors, or to seek a business career.

White, middle-class girls have distinct advantages over those from racial and ethnic minorities and the lower classes. They not only have greater resources and are more likely to attend college (if only to find a husband), but most of them learn about business from their fathers, husbands, male relatives, and male friends. Other possible role models or prime motivators for a young woman are a family friend, a neighbor, an adult in an organization in which the girl works or participates, or a college professor or administrator (usually in a school with a large enrollment of female students, since, according to some academicians, excess of male students in the classroom causes female students to take a back seat and compete less).

Women executives rarely serve as role models. As Margaret Hennig confirmed in her study, these women seldom make an effort to help other women in their companies—and they acknowledge that they suffer from the Queen Bee syndrome (discussed in Chapter 1).

Eli Ginzberg, professor of economics at Columbia University and human resources expert, points out that mothers are largely responsible for the low aspirations of their daughters, and further that "men who are prejudiced against women and discriminate against them are the sons of women. Therefore, women face the challenge of doing a better job of raising their sons, not only as potential employers of women, but as future husbands who will encourage and support their wives' work aspirations." [7]

Husbands are a dominant factor in the making and breaking of women's careers. The disintegration of a marital relationship—with or without separation and divorce—motivates many wives to work, especially if there are children and the husband is not a "good provider." And statistics reveal that more and more women are entering the job market via this route. Here are some of the facts:

- There are fewer "old maids" today, and it is estimated that by the 1980s only about 3 percent of women will remain unmarried.
- Not only are more wives working, but more mothers are, espe-

cially those with younger children. In recent years, the most rapid gains in labor force participation have occurred among wives under 35, especially those with children under 6.[8]

- The divorce rate has been steadily climbing. Between 1960 and 1969, the rate for couples with no children under 18 increased 37 percent, and 62 percent for those with children under 18.[9]

- More couples are separating and living apart; they feel less obligated to stay together because of the children when they themselves are unhappy.

In the marriages that succeed, husbands are more likely to be supportive of wives who work or have careers, or who attend college or take courses to prepare for a career, than husbands were a generation ago.

MAKING IT IN THE MALE WORLD

Let us now consider the dominant characteristics of women who succeed in organizations.

Risk-taking ability. Increasingly, career-oriented women are demonstrating their willingness and ability to take the risk of entering fields and occupations that are traditionally male-dominated. Such pioneering can be a lonely venture. Here are four examples of women who have succeeded in atypical jobs: Maria A. Curry has an engineering degree and is sales and technical manager of the magnetic tape department of Agfa-Gevaert, Inc. Millington F. McCoy is a high-level executive recruiter for Handy Associates. She is one of the few women recruiters in a major search firm. Harriet Michel is executive director of the New York Foundation. Lynn Manka is merchandising manager for *Fortune* magazine. All four women are in their 30s. Some other atypical jobs held by women we talked with: consultant, sales manager, insurance broker, product manager, and several jobs in engineering.

How does a woman reach a high-status, high-profile, one-of-a-kind position? Aside from the basics of ambition, motivation, education, and experience, she does it by sticking her neck out and taking risks. For example:

—She stifles her qualms about how well she'll handle more responsibility, unusual tasks, a chance to speak before a group inside or outside the company—and she does it.

—If she is given an opportunity to take a job never before held by a woman, she grabs it, even though she realizes she has only a 50-50 chance of succeeding.

—If she has too little responsibility or salary in her present job, she directly or indirectly asks her boss for more. If she is turned down, she persists.

—When she is in a job she does well and enjoys, but which offers no possibilities for promotion, she leaves it for a more promising job.

—If she finds she is being consistently shot down, campaigned against, or harassed by someone in her department or company, she takes measures to change the situation.

Don't for a minute assume that an ambitious woman always shows her claws. She may not be an outspoken, conspicuous superwoman; she may camouflage her daring under a pleasant "feminine" exterior—if she can manage it.

Candor. After men experience working with a woman as a peer for the first time, they often say that communication was freer and more open than when they worked only with men. In dealing with male executives, Millie McCoy surmises that she achieves a greater openness with them than a man would achieve, probably because they do not regard her as a threat. She knows it isn't altogether complimentary that her male contacts don't genuinely see her as an equal, but she doesn't get hung up over such attitudes—especially when they enhance the success of her work.

Perhaps one reason that successful career women are able to communicate so candidly is that they have to do quite a bit of leveling with themselves and persons close to them when they decide to undertake the difficulties—hard work, late hours, travel, and so on—required for them to achieve success. They have to answer such questions as "Do I really want this?" and "Is it worth the sacrifices?" And in so doing, they tend to view themselves and others far more realistically than many men do.

High self-esteem. Above all, an aspiring woman must place a high value on herself—her intelligence, abilities, and potential—in order to succeed. Otherwise she won't be able to convince a boss that she deserves a promotion and more money. She must like herself, have confidence in her ability to do a job, take pride in her accomplishments, and value herself highly in relation to others in the marketplace (and in personal relationships as well)—all of which means she does not need to seek approval from others and won't allow others to take advantage of her.

In some women who have reached the top, their self-assurance can be so pronounced that it is offensive to their co-workers. These women are often seen as "unfeminine" and emasculating. Women who succeed must really like themselves a great deal in order to withstand all the negative reactions they provoke in some men, and even in some women.

Ambition. Many young women today are ambitious, but the things they hope to achieve vary. Some divorced women told us they were attracted to a job with a high salary because they needed the money to support their children. Other women had a strong personal desire for economic security. Still others, coming from low- or moderate-income families, said the money was needed in the home.

But many of the women with whom we talked came from upper- and middle-income families in which extra money and financial independence were not necessities. These women were ambitious for other reasons. Many of them were encouraged by their families or inspired by successful, doting fathers. In these cases, the women wanted to gain recognition and status, to prove themselves (to their fathers), to be independent (from their mothers), and, sometimes, to have a different life style. Different women want different things, and successful women usually have very definite ideas about what they want.

High energy level. Most upwardly mobile women who have worked for any length of time realize that if they want to succeed, they have to work harder and smarter, put in longer hours, and do a better job than men who have the same job. And what they get in return is less money and less recognition.

Before the current wave of anti-discrimination, it was very common for a woman, when being offered a job previously held by a man, to be told that one of the reasons the manager wanted her to accept was that he would be getting more for his money. Working wives and mothers often were (and some still are) expected to put in eight or nine hours at their jobs plus another three to four hours of housework. High-potential women, like high-potential men, almost always have tremendous energy and drive. And they utilize this energy by getting more accomplished during the day, staying in the office later, taking work home, and outperforming their co-workers. These are attributes that build careers.

Competitiveness. What is very noticeable in talking with successful women is that while they are assertive and competitive, most of them are not hostile, nor do they direct their competitiveness against any specific persons or groups. Harriet Michel, of the New York Foundation, admits she is very aggressive, so much so that she has never felt "oppressed" as a woman. "But I don't see getting ahead as a *fight,*" she says.

It is likely that the competitive qualities displayed by organizational achievers are based on their firm belief in their own capabilities rather than on other persons' inferiority. They are not seeking to put men in their place or to prove that women are inherently superior to men. Monica de Hellerman, who was a vice president of a financial publishing house and who now runs her own public relations consulting firm, says that if the female executive seems more fiercely competitive than the male, it is because a woman has to be more ambitious and have more drive than a man. However, she adds, women don't have a very good chance of really making it big in the organizational world, because men won't permit them widespread success. Her formula for success is to get business and leadership experience in an organization and then to form your own company.

Women who manifest most of their competitiveness against others of their own sex are practicing a brand of antifeminism similar to that of the male stereotype. But many of them are beginning to realize that women who don't work for the advancement of other women may in the long run stunt their own career progress. Being the one woman in an otherwise all-male group may be flattering, but it is not always the most advantageous arrangement.

Mary Gray, manager of administrative services of Thiokol Chemical Corporation, says that one of the most frequently observed mistakes women make in trying to get ahead is that they lose compassion for other people. Gray feels that a woman is more likely to bring compassion to the work scene than a man and that it is to her advantage to hold on to it. In fact, it is possible that some women lose compassion because they don't want male colleagues to criticize them for being soft.

Healthy attitude about being female. Some women feel an ambivalence about being female: they enjoy certain advantages of being female, yet they feel guilty for using these advantages. It is interesting that a large number of the successful women we interviewed did not seem to suffer from this ambivalence. Harriet Michel once served as assistant to John Lindsay, when he was mayor of New York City. She is convinced that she was recruited because she is black and female, and it doesn't bother her. She is happy to have had the experience.

Mary Gray of Thiokol says a woman can be more blunt than a man. Another woman believes that a woman can often learn faster than a man because she can show her ignorance and ask "dumb questions"—something most men hesitate to do because they feel it would damage their image.

All of the outstanding women indicated that they like other women, relate easily to them, and have women friends—another manifestation of their comfort with being female.

Ease in relating to men. It may come as a surprise to men and women of the "old school," but successful businesswomen are unusually adept in establishing rapport with men. Many of these women talk to a man with warmth and spontaneity even if they have just met. Some women admitted to having worked hard through the years to put men at ease. One manager says that when she travels by plane she does not hesitate to sit beside interesting-looking men and talk to them. "Most men are too shy," she says. "A woman has to help them through it." Another woman executive confirmed this. "For years I went to professional meetings and each night had to eat alone. I used to get so uptight about the fact that almost none of the men I'd been with all day would ask me to join them for dinner. Finally I just got sick of waiting. At one meeting I went up to a man I'd enjoyed talking with during the sessions and asked him if he'd like to have dinner so we could continue our chat. He was a bit shocked, but we had dinner . . . and I've kicked myself ever since for waiting so long to ask a man out.''

Most women feel that it is to their advantage to make the men they meet feel more at ease. They know that men are conditioned to not treat women as equals. Instead of trying to ignore it, says Maria Curry of Agfa-Gevaert, it is best to anticipate and deal with it. When she calls on a potential male customer, his initial reaction is usually amazement to hear her talk in technical terms. Acceptance doesn't follow; rather, the man usually adopts an attitude of ''let's wait and see if she knows what she is talking about.'' That phase may last for two or three meetings, and, in Maria's words, ''it is not pleasant.'' But when she finally does get acceptance and trust, the business relationship can be a sound one.

While such rituals are not pleasant, many women say they have begun to work their way through them without allowing themselves to become uptight or resentful. Many agree with Millie McCoy that it will take at least another generation before men and women begin to free themselves from traditional conditioning.

OBSTACLES TO SUCCESS

Some of the women we talked with were not successful in the organizations in which they worked. Here are some of the factors that hampered their progress.

Lack of specific career goals. To some extent, this is a reflection of our times. Young people no longer feel they must make basic career decisions by the third year of college. And increasingly, middle-aged men and women are discovering that there is no inherent virtue in continuing to work at something that doesn't give them pleasure and satisfaction.

Nevertheless, when a woman has only a vague idea about where she wants to go in her career, she may appear to have the previously mentioned characteristics of passivity, dependency, and so on. A man presenting the same kind of thinking would probably be considered immature. But he wouldn't be stereotyped, as a woman is.

Many women enter a particular field or industry without considering whether it is suitable for them or where it will lead them. They lack "career sense"; that is, they are unable to determine where their best opportunities for upward mobility are. Young women commonly make the mistake of entering the teaching field, even though it is already full, and ignoring the occupations and professions (such as computer systems and engineering) which have a variety of jobs available and pay higher salaries.

Failure to channel resentment over discrimination. This factor is perhaps best described by one female professional talking about a colleague: "She spends most of her time worrying about how she is treated on the job and too damn little about being productive." It is an extreme case, but the consciousness of women is rising, and there are bound to be some whose concern with their rights takes priority over achieving success in their careers. And in most organizations this priority doesn't score.

Many successful women have found ways to use their resentment over discrimination to increase their ambition, drive, and determination. Not that strong emotional reactions to being considered second-class citizens aren't justified—they are, and they're normal. But a woman who permits these negative feelings to interfere with her performance is hampering her own progress.

Failure to resolve role conflicts. This difficulty is exemplified by the many women who need or seek their husbands' approval in order to launch or proceed with their careers. When one of these women, a talented copywriter, was given a raise that made her salary higher than that of her husband, he objected and pressured her to stop working. To avoid marital conflict, she actually did quit, but her problems were not solved because she continues to be very resentful about having given up her job.

From the characteristics we've observed in talking with women who have climbed the organizational ladder—and those who have not—we have not come up with a hard-and-fast formula for success. Unquestionably, observation of men and women who are making it to the top can point to those attitudes, behaviors, and skills that are held in the highest regard in many organizations. But we are not suggesting that the way to the top is slavish imitation of those who have succeeded. The ambitious woman will have to work with the ingredients within *herself*—and the help she can get from outside.

REFERENCES

1. Cynthia Fuchs Epstein, *Woman's Place: Options and Limits in Professional Careers* (Berkeley: University of California Press, 1971), p. 66.
2. Estelle Ramey, "She Is Woman," *The New York Times,* September 24, 1973, p. 33.
3. Jane W. Torrey, "A Psychologist's Look at Women," *Journal of Contemporary Business,* Summer 1973, p. 32. Excerpted from *The Johns Hopkins Magazine.*
4. Margaret Hennig, "Career Development for Women Executives," doctoral dissertation, Harvard University, 1970.
5. Marilyn Bender, "A Profile of the Woman Boss," *The New York Times,* February 21, 1971, pp. 49–50.
6. Sandra M. Brown, "The Executive Suite: What Gets You There," *The Executive Woman,* October 1973, p. 5.
7. Eli Ginzberg and Alice M. Yohalem (eds.), *Corporate Lib: Women's Challenge to Management* (Baltimore: The Johns Hopkins University Press, 1973), p. 144.
8. Elizabeth Waldman and Robert Whitmore, "Children of Working Mothers, March 1973," *Monthly Labor Review,* May 1974, p. 51.
9. Ibid.

3

PERSONAL ASSESSMENT AND LIFE PLANNING

A FRIEND was involved in making a job change and was kicking around the idea of switching to another industry. At our suggestion, we arranged to have lunch with an acquaintance, an extremely personable multi-function, multi-industry executive, to get his opinion about which fields would be most promising and to discuss what our friend should do next.

We met for lunch and after about an hour of animated conversation, the executive held up his hand and said, "Wait a minute, I think you're on the wrong track. You've been asking, 'What are my best career paths?' and 'What kind of job should I go after next?' But you should be asking yourself these questions: 'What kind of life do I want? How and where do I want to live?' "

Our friend, a Harvard MBA, was startled because life choices hadn't even crossed his mind; in fact, the career choices he had been considering were very limited. He was planning to job-hunt in two or three industries, select the job and industry that looked most promising, and let the other aspects of his life fall into place as his career developed. The possibilities of not having a corporate career or of entering a nonprofit field had never occurred to him.

OVERCOMING PERSONAL OBSTACLES

Many women share our friend's shortcoming: they don't really plan their lives; they involve themselves in the selection of a college, a mate, a job. Few of them decide that they want to achieve certain things during their lifetime (other than being a wife and a mother), and then prepare themselves so they have the necessary qualifications, and afterward go out and get what they want.

If you want to plan your life, here are some steps you'll need to take:

1. Perceive yourself as an individual. Most girls and women see themselves as women first and individuals or human beings second, just as most men are primarily concerned about what they are as men. But this is changing. The liberated woman no longer accepts the premise that she is so different from men that she cannot participate in the same types of activities and have a similar life style. She wants first to be accepted and to be treated as a human being, not as a woman—and certainly not as a traditional woman.

2. Seek recognition and status. A woman is usually asked "What does your husband do?" instead of "What do you do?" And if her husband has a professional or executive position, she is usually proud to state what he does, because she identifies closely with his career, even if she has a career of her own.

However, women are beginning to seek the recognition and status they deserve. As Elizabeth Janeway notes: "The long-term trend reveals a marked shift in the image of women that emerges: women are more and more seen as approaching the capable, active, involved human norm and leaving 'otherness' behind. Their interests grow wider. They are assumed to arrive at their own decisions more frequently. They stop being adjuncts of parents or husbands." [1]

3. Take more initiative. Most women aren't sufficiently action-oriented. Instead of being doers, they are done to. They are used to having fathers and husbands and bosses make decisions for them. Some working wives still turn over their paychecks to their husbands and have all their purchases supervised.

Because girls are discouraged from striking out on their own at the same time their brothers are being pushed into being independent, many need some sort of special guidance counseling or training.

Since special programs and courses designed for women have only recently become available, one often hears older women offer younger ones this kind of advice: "You have to be tough, work harder and longer hours, but, more than that, you have to work smarter than other people. And that means seizing opportunities and acting on them before anyone else does."

4. Think about your career early. Girls who start thinking about careers at a young age and who assume from childhood that they will work because their mothers do, or because their fathers want them to, have an obvious advantage, as we have already mentioned. But what about the others? When they go to college, do they realize that they are handicapped—not just because they are females but because they are undermotivated and too complacent during childhood and adolescence? No, they seldom realize it at this stage. Only when they graduate and enter the job market do they become aware of it, and then many of them feel it is too late to do anything about their situation.

But they are absolutely wrong. A number of ambitious women are heading right back to school. They enroll in night courses or in an MBA program if they can afford it. Some have to work a few years before they can afford more college, yet they do it. Instead of spending their money on other things, they use it on their education because they know they will be more than reimbursed in the future.

5. Invest to get a return on your capabilities. Follow the example set by the women enrolling in MBA programs, and the increasing numbers who are entering college to become professionals. Invest your money and time in ways that will contribute to your career and

your life. Far too few women are devoting time to reading business periodicals and books, to planning a job-hunting campaign, or to learning about the company or industry in which they work.

There are other ways you should invest in yourself. Keep up with the latest developments in your field. Make investments for your later years—not just in stock, which a number of women buy, but in a personal pension program, a house or real estate, or life insurance. Develop skills that will enable you to do freelance work for extra income and part-time work when you are retired. And, if possible, save money to tide you over in case you want to make a job change, or return to college, or are suddenly faced with an emergency.

6. Learn to make informed choices. It's not just a matter of deciding to take this job or that one at a given time but of making major decisions about your life and career, gathering relevant information about feasible options and opportunities, considering all the key determinants, and reaching conclusions about what should be done.

Today women have many more alternatives to choose among, and much more information about them. Inform yourself about new areas opening up for women and new college programs and job opportunities. The next step is to evaluate these options, assessing your capabilities, setting your goals, and developing a career plan for yourself.

METHODS OF ASSESSING YOUR STRENGTHS AND WEAKNESSES

Whether your job fits in with your career plans or you'd like to leave it for something more challenging and more appropriate, you should "take a reading" of yourself—your assets and liabilities— periodically. There are several different assessment methods that you might use.

The first method is a brief quiz prepared by Edith M. Lynch for her book *The Executive Suite—Feminine Style*.[2] It can help you determine how strongly motivated (and clear-thinking) you are about having a career. Don't just read the questions; write out the answers as you go along. Then review them for the purpose of developing ways you can improve yourself—your attitudes and your behavior—in the areas in which you find yourself to be weak.

1. What do I really think of my own talents?
2. Am I willing to make the most of my talents?
3. Do I resent the fact that men seem to have the best jobs, the best chances of promotion, and the most exciting challenges?
4. How am I trying to improve my own position—more education, more research, better attitude?
5. Do I look at everything emotionally instead of making some well-thought-out plans?
6. When did I last read a book pertaining to the jobs I'd like to hold?
7. Do I continually think of myself as a secretary, as a helper, as a crutch instead of being the actual person doing the higher-level job?
8. Do I pass the blame for not having a good job off on someone else—my parents, the boss, the school I attended, and so on?
9. Am I willing to do the hard work necessary to hold a responsible job?
10. Am I willing to work as a member of a team to accomplish a worthwhile project?
11. Am I willing to help others on the way up, particularly other women?
12. Am I willing to fight for my rights on equal ground and on the basis of what I have done and can do in the future?

Another approach, the comparison method of assessment, is risky. In trying to develop a personal profile, people frequently resort to measuring themselves against others, especially those in similar jobs: how well you (and they) get along with bosses, how popular you are, whether you get the really good opportunities, and what others think of you. However, comparisons of this kind are not at all reliable in determining your true identity. Instead, they can cause you to lose sight of the real you. Here are some of the pitfalls of comparisons:

Minimization. You may tend to focus on the differences between you and your colleagues that are not very significant. How you and they dress, for instance, or who goes to lunch with whom may become a matter of prime importance. The truly important factors—such as education, experience, skills, work attitudes, health, ambitions, perceptions—are often lost in the shuffle.

Exaggeration. You may feel that your co-workers are doing better in their jobs than you are in yours, which may cause you to blow up your deficiencies (or what you feel are your deficiencies) out of all proportion. Conversely, you may unduly inflate what you consider to be a great performance of your own. In either case, you have missed the truth.

Imitation. If you see a co-worker do something very well, you may decide to try imitating him or her. For example, a co-worker may do a great deal of talking at the monthly staff meetings. You believe this contributes to the person's success, and you copy the style—even though your own verbal strength has always been the crisp opinion delivered at the fortuitous moment. Obviously, such behavior only takes you further away from the real you.

Oversensitivity. You may pay too much attention to what others tell you—or to their nonverbal signals—about yourself. Since these opinions are inevitably based on some degree of personal bias (no matter how much you might like to believe otherwise), you are receiving a distorted picture.

Thus, outside criticism of you can lead you to assume you have a major defect in character. And, on the other hand, praise from someone else can have you believing you're a genius. In either case, judgments about yourself based on this feedback will be inaccurate.

It is not an easy job to see yourself clearly. You are so close to yourself that you tend to have blurred vision. However, the complex process of self-evaluation can be simplified somewhat if you follow these steps:

Look at your failures. We're talking about clear-cut failures where there is objective evidence that labels what you did—or did not do—as such. In addition, you may have come out of the experience suspecting that the skills required were beyond your interests and abilities.

Look at your triumphs. Consider those things you have done outstandingly well, the accomplishments that have earned you merited praise. You enjoyed a project, and felt that even though you needed more experience, you were a *natural*.

Determine your assets. This can be done by answering some pointed questions:

—What do you do best? What gives you the most satisfaction? Research? Training? Rewriting? Detailed desk work? Dealing with others? Compiling reports? Statistical work? Public relations?
—What do others frequently call on you to do?
—What things do you do that others no longer try to do because you are so good at them? Have you, for example, been so successful at setting up meetings that no one else now volunteers to do that job?

The point is that what you do best is usually what you like most. And the work others call on you to do, or that they acknowledge you are best at, is further evidence of your particular abilities.

Obviously, your answers are going to be somewhat prejudiced, but they can still provide you with a good deal of objective information about yourself. And they can point you in the direction of the career and goals that are right for you.

How Well Do You Know Yourself?

This is a three-step exercise that some people have used to flesh out the profile of their strengths and weaknesses. It is an exercise that can increase a person's self-confidence and sense of personal worth.

Step one: Imagine you are one of your co-workers. An executive search firm calls you to get more information on your "co-worker" (you, in actuality). They don't specify the kind of job they have in mind, but they ask you to be as candid as possible in assessing all pluses and minuses.

While you are thinking about what you will tell the caller, get a tape or cassette recorder if you can. The idea of making your assessment out loud may not appeal to you at first and may make you feel self-conscious, but the one big advantage it has over the use of pencil and paper is that you'll hear yourself as others hear you, and you'll end up with a new insight into yourself and your resources.

Pick a time and a place in which you won't be interrupted. Then put the recorder on and start talking as if you were addressing the caller from the executive search firm. Talk about what your co-worker does well—and not so well. Comment on what she seems to like—and not to like. For example, discuss:

—Her principal job functions and responsibilities.
—The functions in her previous positions and skills acquired that might be useful to her career progress.
—The tasks she performs that are not an essential part of her job (but which could tell something about her work habits and commitments).
—The functions she appears obviously unsuited to perform.
—Her career ambitions and goals, with comments on how strongly motivated and career-oriented she is. (Does she volunteer for new responsibilities, put in extra hours, seek special training, etc.?)
—Her working habits: Can she handle detail work, meet deadlines, work without close supervision, manage her time, set realistic priorities?
—Her working relationships with superiors, peers, and so forth.
—Her commitment to her work: Does she permit conflicts to arise between personal life and business? (Would she cancel a personal engagement to meet an office deadline?)
—Her communication skills, such as writing and speaking before groups.
—Functions she could perform better if she had more training.
—Kinds of functions and responsibilities that she does not or would not perform due to lack of interest or talent.

Step two: Now, play back the tape and from it make a list of strengths and weaknesses, likes and dislikes. Human nature being what it is, it's likely that your original assessment was not completely candid. As you listen and make notes, it may occur to you that you played down a strength. If so, underline it for emphasis now. Of course, you may have the opposite reaction—that you spent a great deal of time talking about a plus that, on further reflection, doesn't seem all that impressive. In that case, circle it so you can come back to it later and think about why you put so much stress on it.

When you've finished the list, you should realistically assume that you have favored your pluses and underplayed your minuses. To test yourself on this, develop an exaggeration for each strength or preference. For example, if you are time-conscious and see yourself as an excellent time manager, take it one step further. Is it possible that others see you as compulsive, the kind of person who can't stand being five minutes late—and who can't tolerate the slightest lateness in others? If you feel you relate well to others, including strangers, might you relate so well that people who meet you for the first time find you glib? Or if you see yourself as very articulate and well read, consider how well you resist the temptation to dazzle others with your erudition by sprinkling your conversation with obscure literary references and large words that have no meaning to your audience. Look over each exaggeration. Some you can reject. Others you may feel come uncomfortably close to the truth.

Step three: Put a plus next to each strength or skill that others have confirmed in their comments about or to you. Then place minuses by the weaknesses that others have noticed. This adds an element of objectivity to your self-appraisal.

Now that you've developed a list of areas in which you feel you have some qualifications and areas in which you are less skilled, perhaps the first thing you should do is to be starkly realistic about the weaknesses: How important are they to your career? Some qualities that you lack should not be worried about—unless, in your efforts to overcome them, you take time away from areas more vital to your future. If, for instance, you're weak in mathematics, decide honestly if gaining strength in this area is important to your future. If it is, make a note to do something about it. If it isn't, move on to the next area.

There will probably be some weaknesses that you've always intended to do something about. The same applies to your strengths—there may be some that you've never really developed into practical skills. Obviously this doesn't mean that you should embark on a program to eliminate every weakness and develop every skill. The time and money required to turn aptitudes into skills must be considered. If you establish priorities, based on what really interests you and on profitable applications for new strengths, you'll find it easier to take the first steps toward self-development.

Keep in mind that your priorities should be based not only on your career goals, but on the job you have right now. Although your advancement isn't totally dependent on what kind of a job you do at present, your current performance—in which you display some of the abilities you'll need in the future—can play a substantial role in your selection by others for more responsible and more challenging work.

FOCUS YOUR OBJECTIVES

As noted before, many women still are not accustomed to thinking in terms of specific *career* steps. Even if they have some idea of what they'd like to do, they have not determined how they might reach their objectives.

To help develop your own career plans, therefore, you should give some thought to your personal and professional needs. Unfortunately, many people in business take the path of least resistance and put the needs of the organization above their personal objectives. Others make the mistake of relying on the advice of friends or other outsiders. In planning your career, however, it's vital to start with your own needs, which generally correspond to your potential. Only you can determine what you like and do best.

Look again at the profile of your strengths and weaknesses. What kinds of work do you enjoy doing most? What gives you the greatest feeling of accomplishment? What are your goals—to make money? to achieve expertness in a specialty? to acquire responsibility for the work of others? to earn the esteem of your colleagues? to gain power? to be of service to others? Here are some things to do to help you clarify your objectives:

1. Assume you have to quit your job. What is the one thing about the job you hate to give up? Write it down. Then make a note of the second thing you most regret leaving behind, and so on.

2. List the five most important things you do in your job. First rank them in order of importance. Then rank them in order of enjoyment. You might also want to compare these entries with those on your "most hate to give up" list.

3. List the aspects of your job that you talk about most. Put down the things you say when someone asks you to describe your job.

These lists should clue you in to what gratifies you, to what you probably should spend more time doing, and to what potential you have that can be actualized. You can then translate your new knowledge into goals.

In summary, there are three questions you should ask yourself frequently as a form of diagnostic and preventive analysis: What am I doing now that I don't have to do, or don't want to do? What am I *not* doing that I would like to do? Where do I want to be in five years? In ten years?

The answers to these questions, together with the data on yourself that you have already developed from reading this book, will help you keep a sharp eye on where you are and where you're going.

IF YOU'RE MARRIED . . .

More and more women work because they are the only person heading the household and they have to support themselves and their children. During the past few years, several other facts have emerged:

—The greatest percentage increase of working mothers has been among those with children under three years of age.[3]
—The highest percentage increase of divorce has been among couples with four or more children.[4]
—The number of women heads of families increased one-third between March 1962 and March 1972. Of these 6.2 million

females, about 40 percent became widows, 25 percent got divorced, and 20 percent separated from their husbands.[5] The March 1973 figure was 6.6 million.[6]

These statistics suggest that wives and mothers who do not work or who are currently working only to earn supplemental income should give serious consideration to what their situations would be if they were to join the ranks of women who are divorced, separated, or widowed now or some time in the future. If this happened to you, would you be prepared to go out and get a job? Could you support yourself and your children? If not, what are you going to do about it?

Douglas Basil, professor of management at the University of Southern California, has stated:

> The divorce rate is high and there seems to be no indication that it will decline in the years ahead. Women may find that they are not able to be fulfilled in marriage sufficiently and that they must seek the challenge of work and a management career. This is not to deprecate marriage as an institution or to consider that many if not the majority of women may still prefer the traditional marriage to maintaining a career with or without marriage.[7]

Basil believes that because of the "fragile qualities of marriage" young women should be encouraged to seek job experience that will permit them to attain managerial positions and that they should be discouraged from marrying early.

Perhaps you don't need to be convinced that you should prepare for a career, but you're married to a man who is somewhat traditional (though he may deny it), and you're concerned about how he is going to react to your making a transition and a commitment to a career. Even if you've carefully mentioned the subject and he seems agreeable to the idea, you may still be wondering how he's going to react to cooking his own dinner, running the vacuum, and assuming some of the other household chores.

At some point you'll probably have to face the fact that you can't possibly manage a career unless your husband is supportive. You then have the alternatives of discussing openly with him the changes that are bound to occur, or of gently breaking him into his new supportive role. That is, the choice appears to be between taking a this-is-the-way-things-are stance and teaching him on the installment plan. Actually, for most husbands the most effective approach is probably a combination of the two.

Couples, especially those with professional or administrative occupations, may work out a special career pattern that is agreeable to both partners. Instead of each spouse pursuing a separate career, the couple may choose one of the following arrangements:

Joint careers: Husband and wife are in the same professional or business occupation, and they either work in the same organization, such as doctors in the same hospital or lawyers in the same law firm, or they work together in their own office or home.

Compatible careers: The spouses have separate occupations in the same field; for example, doctor and nurse, engineer and architect, architect and interior decorator, marketing consultant and market researcher.

Team careers: Husband and wife work for the same organization as a team. When the organization promotes or transfers them, the change is made for them as a team. This approach is practiced by the U.S. State Department for its foreign service personnel.

Reversed traditional roles: The wife works from 9:00 to 5:00 and the husband stays home. The husband may write, may be a professional with an office at home, may attend college or graduate school, or may simply devote most of his time to running the household. This arrangement was almost nonexistent a generation ago, but today some couples are finding it the one that works best for them.

Geographically separated occupations: Spouses work in organizations that are a significant distance from each other, making it necessary for them to live apart for days, weeks, or months at a time.

Many universities, companies, and other organizations have policies against hiring husbands and wives. Only a few actually encourage members of the same family to work in the same organization and location, and they usually do not permit them to work in the same department.

If a firm is relocating an employee, it will sometimes help that person's spouse to find a job in the new location. But when a man is being transferred, most companies simply assume that his wife and children will go with him when he moves. They're not prepared to cope with problems that can arise when these men have career wives.

Regardless of the policies of organizations, there seems to be a trend among young men and women to form partnerships, rather than superior-subordinate relationships, and to carry this into their careers. Eli Ginzberg has observed that more and more young couples are planning their life and work careers jointly. He notes the intriguing development that more male graduate students are interested in performing voluntary activities outside their jobs (or even within them if the company will permit it), while more female graduates are leaving voluntary work and trying to get into the world of paid work. Ginzberg has remarked:

> What happens to women is very much a function of how men change. That means primarily fathers and husbands. As I see it, there is more and more coupled planning for life. That is, it used to be understood that the only person whose career was important was the man because he was the only one who could make a decent living. The woman went along for the ride and she sort of fitted in whatever work she did depending on the man's requirement.[8]

With so many developments favoring women and joint career planning, Dr. Ginzberg believes it is quite possible that well-educated men with a comfortable income may eventually enjoy the same options now enjoyed by educated, higher-income women, such as those of when to work, how much to work, and under what conditions to work.

PLANNING YOUR LIFE AND CAREER

Men tend to suffer far less from the consequences of poor planning and decision making than women because the system in which we live and work was designed by men for men, so it functions to their advantage. In his book on male chauvinism, Michael Korda points out that "in most offices, men control, administer, decide upon the security and futures of countless women. The reverse is very seldom true." Furthermore, he says that women are cheap labor, are thought of as replaceable, and are seldom given the training that would make them more valuable. "Men have arrogated to themselves the enormous advantages of continuity; they have a sense, however illusory, of permanency. Women rarely do, except in the sad sense of having stayed too long, of having abandoned all their other options, being left at the age of fifty the untrained and unwelcome ward of some corporation." [9]

In the cold light of reality, it becomes apparent that women need to predetermine what they are going to do with their lives, so they can acquire the education, training, and experience necessary for them to achieve success within the framework of male-dominated organizations.

REFERENCES

1. Elizabeth Janeway, "The Weak Are the Second Sex," *Atlantic Monthly,* December 1973, p. 96.
2. Edith M. Lynch, *The Executive Suite—Feminine Style* (New York: AMACOM, 1973), pp. 221–222.
3. Howard Hayghe, "Marital and Family Characteristics of the Labor Force in March 1973," *Monthly Labor Review,* April 1974, p. 24.
4. Elizabeth Waldman and Robert Whitmore, "Children of Working Mothers, March 1973," *Monthly Labor Review,* May 1974, p. 51.
5. "Facts about Women Heads of Households and Heads of Families" (Washington, D.C.: U.S. Department of Labor, Women's Bureau, April 1973), pp. 3–4.
6. Howard Hayghe, op. cit.
7. Douglas C. Basil, *Women in Management* (New York: Dunellen, 1972), p. 111.
8. Eli Ginzberg, in *Women's Work Has Just Begun.* Report on the Conference on the Redesigning of Work, The New School, New York, September 17, 1973, pp. 9, 12.
9. Michael Korda, *Male Chauvinism! How It Works* (New York: Random House, 1973), p. 83.

4

YOUR PRIMARY ASSETS– EDUCATION, MONEY, AND YOU

THE basic concerns of women embarking on careers are not so different from those of men starting out. They worry about how attractive they are to the persons they want to impress, about whether they have the qualifications required to get the type of job they want, and about whether they can make their income stretch far enough to pay the rent and buy food, clothing, and other essentials.

At present, these concerns are especially valid for women, since they are less likely to have a clear-cut idea of the kind of impression they should make, an education that provides specific job skills and knowledge, and enough money in the bank to tide them over while they job-hunt.

To more experienced persons these concerns may seem to be highly personal, short-lived problems that everyone goes through and therefore not worth discussing. Let us assure you, they are important. You may not have suffered through this experience, but many women have: you visit a company for a job interview, and soon after you are introduced to and start talking with the manager whose stamp of approval you require, you realize that you are all wrong—your résumé, your clothes, your personality. He is sophisticated and you feel like a gawky teenager.

It takes time to develop an air of assurance and a look of success. Eventually you find out that many people who act and sound as if they come from affluent families really don't. You learn to wear appropriate clothes (conservative ones), to look people straight in the eye and give them a firm handshake when you meet them, and to avoid behaving aggressively and talking too loudly. But all this takes time and effort. We hope that the information in this chapter will help women start out, or get back, on the right track to using their assets to their best advantage.

EDUCATION

Edith Head, the famous Hollywood designer, stated in the foreword of Douglas Basil's book *Women in Management:*

> Education is the greatest prerequisite for success for any woman. In my own case, although I am now a designer for the movie industry and my formal education was not in design, the scholastic preparation that I obtained in the university provided me with the confidence and understanding necessary for my life-long career.[1]

College for Edith Head was a confidence-building experience, not a skills-building one. And what she says about the importance of education is true. But the woman who wants a career today must have an education that provides her with skills. A liberal arts degree is no longer such a good thing to have. The consensus of businesswomen, academicians, and recruiters is that women must have a college education which prepares them to work, which provides them with occupational or professional skills and knowledge needed in the job market. A woman should select a field in which there is (and will be) a demand; study it in college, getting at least one degree but preferably two; and then get the experience necessary to become an expert in the field.

Enrollment in MBA Programs and Professional Schools

During the past few years company recruiters have begun to hunt aggressively for women with degrees in accounting, engineering, business administration, and data processing. The demand for women lawyers has increased, and acceptance of women in the fields of pharmacy, dentistry, and medicine has grown. The result has been a tremendous increase in the number of women seeking and gaining admission to professional schools and colleges of business administration.

For example, in 1967 only 2,505 women were enrolled in engineering schools; in 1972 there were 5,317. The number of female law students rose from 3,306 in 1967 to 12,728 in 1972. In terms of total enrollment, these five-year figures show increases of from 1 percent to 3 percent of the total engineering students, and from 5 percent up to 12 percent of the total law students.[2]

The jump in enrollment has been even greater in some schools of business administration. At Columbia University, 20 percent of the 1973 class entering the Graduate School of Business were women, compared with only a handful of women who entered a decade ago.[3] And a West Coast university reported that 17 percent of the 300 students enrolling in its MBA program were women.

Universities are offering some new programs, such as joint business/law degrees and engineering BS/MBA degrees (a highly desirable combination), but the most promising developments are in the college programs for women and nontraditional areas described below. Before we turn to that, however, here are three good reference books, available in paperback, if you need some general information about the traditional colleges: *The New York Times Guide to College Selection,* by Ella Mazel (Quadrangle Books, 1972, $4.95); *Einstein's College Entrance Guide,* by Bernice Einstein (Grosset & Dunlap, 1971, $4.95); and *Comparative Guide to American Colleges,* by James Cass and Max Birnbaum (Harper & Row, 1973, $5.95).

Colleges Without Walls

Universities have always offered opportunities to work toward a degree during summer sessions or at night, but many adults have been discouraged from pursuing degrees by the lack of suitable programs for their particular circumstances. Neither the course content nor the method of study was designed for the education of adults, especially those who worked during the day and studied for a degree at night.

Now this situation has changed. Stimulated by the phenomenal success of Great Britain's Open University, founded in 1969, and propelled by social changes, the educational community started to generate nontraditional types of programs, which are now becoming more widely available.

The new programs represent a broad range of educational methods. For example, some require regular class attendance, whereas others have no campus and no classrooms; some have a prescribed curriculum, while others are unstructured; some measure a student's competence by examinations, and others rely on a general assessment by the student's academic adviser; some set no time limit for completion of credits needed for a degree, but others establish a certain number of years as the limit for completion.

Features common to many of the new programs, however, are: individualized curricula, encouragement of independent study guided by tutors or advisers, and a contractual agreement between the adviser and student, specifying the course of study and the requirements to be met to attain a degree.

Although the field is too new for a definitive description, the following five projects will give you an idea of the kinds of programs available:

Empire State College: This is a new unit of the State University of New York. It has no campus. Students go to "learning centers" (which are now being established in various localities) to meet with their advisers. Together, they develop "learning contracts," which set out flexible programs adapted to the student's needs. Both associate and bachelor's degrees are offered. For their bulletin, write to Empire State College, Saratoga Springs, N.Y. 12866.

New York Regents External Degree Program: Started in fall 1970 by the New York State Education Department, this program offers three degrees: bachelor of business, associate in arts, and associate in nursing. Any person, including individuals from out of state, can obtain a degree by taking standard proficiency tests or oral, written, or performance exams and meeting specified requirements. There are no prescribed methods by which the student learns; all kinds of educational activities are encouraged. Write to Division of Independent Study, State Education Department, 99 Washington Avenue, Albany, N.Y. 12210.

Minnesota Metropolitan State College: Established in June 1971, this urban college has no campus, but uses facilities and resources of the community. It concentrates on undergraduate and graduate programs for persons with two years of college or the equivalent. Students work under contracts that specify degree requirements, formal courses, and independent studies to be carried out. Degrees offered include bachelor in engineering, administration, and liberal arts, and professional masters. Request information from Minnesota Metropolitan State College, St. Paul Coordinating Center, 421 North Wabasha Street, St. Paul, Minn. 55102.

California State College External Degree Programs: Several upper- and lower-level programs were initiated in 1971; Chico State and six community colleges are cooperating in "external programs" under which working adults can obtain bachelor of arts degrees in administration and other fields. Programs are to be offered in Bakersfield (BS, business), Dominquez Hills (MBA), and other locations. However, many of these degrees are currently available only to residents of the areas. For information, write to the Commission on External Degree Programs, 1801 East Cotati Avenue, Rohnert Park, Calif. 94928; request "The 1,000 Mile Campus."

University Without Walls: Started in 1971, when 3,000 students were enrolled, this project is being conducted by 20 colleges and universities in more than a dozen states. Students have no prescribed curriculum or uniform time schedule for completing a degree, but instead follow programs, tailor-made by them and their advisers. They learn through a variety of methods: apprenticeship, independent study, travel, programmed instruction, and regular course work.

The participating institutions include: University of Alabama, Antioch College, Baltimore Community College, Bard College, Chicago State College, Florida International, Friends World College, Goddard College, Howard University, Loretto Heights College, University of Massachusetts, University of Minnesota, Morgan State College, New College at Sarasota, New York University, Northeastern Illinois State College, University of Oklahoma, Park College, Roger Williams College, Shaw University, Skidmore College, University of South Carolina, Staten Island Community College, and Stephens College.

Write to Union for Experimenting Colleges and Universities, Antioch College, Yellow Springs, Ohio 45387 for details.

Information about programs offered by other institutions is available in two directories: *Increasing the Options: Recent Developments in College and University Degree Programs,* by John R. Valley (Office of New Degree Programs, Educational Testing Service, Princeton, N.J. 08540, $2.50); and *The New York Times Guide to Continuing Education in America,* edited by Frances Coombs Thomson (prepared for the College Entrance Examination Board, Quadrangle Books, 330 Madison Ave., New York, N.Y. 10017, $12.50).

Fast Track to a College Degree

If you have one or more years of college and, even though you're working, you are really eager to accumulate more credits so you can get a bachelor's degree, you should investigate CLEP, the College Level Examination Program. Established in 1965 as an activity of the College Entrance Examination Board, the program enables people to take examinations and, if they pass, to get college credits without taking formal courses. Over 1,200 colleges and universities all over the United States now offer college credit on the basis of CLEP scores—about three times the number of only two years ago.

At least 700 of these colleges and universities administer the tests on campus. There are two kinds of tests: (1) five general examinations that measure college-level achievement in English composition, mathematics, natural sciences, humanities, social sciences, and history, and (2) thirty-four subject examinations that measure achievement in specific college courses such as accounting, business law, business management, computer programming, and marketing.

Examinations are held during the third week of every month at all test centers except Washington, D.C., where tests are given on any weekday throughout the year for an extra $5. The fees for general examinations are $15 for one and $25 for two to five; subject examinations are $15 each. Persons who live more than 100 miles from the nearest center may request a "special administration" at a more convenient location for an additional $10. Applicants must register at least three weeks prior to the exam. Test scores are mailed to the candidate and to the college or university she specifies on the registration form.

The scores for which credit is awarded are determined solely by the individual colleges and universities, not by CLEP. Therefore, an applicant for CLEP should first find out whether the exams she intends to take meet the specific requirements of her chosen university, how many credits can be received for which exams, and what grades must be attained. She should also inquire about time limitations and whether the college charges any fees for granting credits. Further information can be obtained by writing to CLEP, College Entrance Examination Board, P.O. Box 592, Princeton, N.J. 08540.

College Programs for Women

Colleges have been adding job-related and skills-related courses, work/study programs, and special counseling to meet women's needs for advanced education. Radcliffe, one of the "seven sister" women's colleges in the Northeast, which have been traditionally liberal-arts oriented, is a forerunner of business administration programs for women. Radcliffe's graduate program is taught by Harvard professors, and its students have been sought after by large companies for quite a few years. (Several of the women with whom we talked graduated from this program.)

Of the other sister colleges, Barnard has established a women's center to counsel and assist women inside and outside the college, as well as an internship program for sophomores and juniors. The program was originally made possible by the efforts of alumnae who arranged for students to spend a month on the job in a New York City firm—in one case at a woman's monthly magazine, in another at a public relations firm. Sarah Lawrence has set up a center for continuing education to encourage women who have been out of school for four or more years to return to study for degrees.

Women have been very involved in the development of continuing education. In 1966 Elizabeth Cless co-founded the Minnesota Plan of the State University, which was a pioneer of the 500 continuing education programs designed for women in the past decade.

According to the Women's Bureau of the U.S. Department of Labor, there are special education programs for "mature women" (over 35) in all but four states—Alaska, Nevada, South Dakota, and Wyoming—and four out of every ten colleges and universities have these programs. Approximately 40 institutions offer "nontraditional" studies that are nonmatriculating; that is, they don't lead to a degree.

Cless, who served on the task force of the National Coalition for Research on Women's Education and Development, stated that "community colleges have done the most for women. Next comes the four-year college. Universities have done the least."

Women's groups in Boston and Brooklyn have conducted some detailed studies on their college communities in order to recommend changes in women's programs. The Boston group has put out a handbook that explains how to choose a program, how to apply to a college, where to get financial aid, and so on; it is called *The Urban Woman's Guide to Higher Education,* published by WIN-NERS, the Women's Inner-City Educational Resource Service, a grassroots counseling service.

Simmons College has a special graduate business administration program that will confer a master's degree. Pace University is embarking on a program to prepare women with liberal arts degrees for business, through an MBA program, internship, and counseling. The University of Missouri's Discovery Program for Women provides career counseling, self-assessment, and upgrading of management skills.

There are many other programs, and you can survey the field with a copy of *Continuing Education Programs and Services for Women,* which lists schools throughout the country. It may be obtained through the Women's Bureau of the Department of Labor, or the Superintendent of Documents, Government Printing Office, Washington, D.C. 20402.

A variety of correspondence courses are available for home study. Extension divisions of universities call them independent study. You can acquire college credits from institutions that belong to the National University Extension Association. To obtain a list of undergraduate courses offered by more than 50 colleges and universities, write to the National University Extension Association, University of Minnesota, Room 112, Building TSMC, Minneapolis, Minn. 55455.

Some college credits are available through programmed instruction and television courses. For information, write to The National Society for Programmed Instruction, Trinity University, 715 Stadium Drive, San Antonio, Tex. 78212.

AWARE, the Association for Women's Active Return to Education, may be able to provide some assistance through local chapters. Write to AWARE, 5820 Wilshire Boulevard, Suite 605, Los Angeles, Calif. 90036.

MONEY

A career woman undergoes an almost endless series of money problems, ranging from how to gracefully pay for a man's lunch to how to convince officers of a bank to extend her a mortgage. Actually some women begin to experience problems in this area even before they get to the career point: they find that educational costs are just as high for women as for men, but there are fewer places where women can borrow money to pay those costs, fewer scholarships and fellowships available, fewer part-time jobs that pay enough money to work and go to school at the same time.

Develop a Good Credit Rating

As soon as a woman gets a job that pays a salary, she is well advised to start building a good credit rating. And the best way to do this is to go into debt—a manageable debt. These days it isn't realistic to follow the Calvinistic tradition that some of our parents and grandparents followed: you don't buy anything unless you can pay cash for it. Young women today who follow this tradition find that when they want to borrow money for a major expenditure—education, car, furniture—they have no credit rating. Here are some recommendations for establishing a good credit rating:

Borrow a small amount of money, preferably from a large bank, even though you don't need it. The advantages of a large bank are its wider range of services, well-known name, and branches in other areas.

Apply for a bank identification card, a check cashing card, or a cash payment card at your bank. That way you can cash checks, usually at any of the bank's branches, without having to obtain an officer's okay.

Establish charge accounts at the larger and better-known department stores in your area. Use these accounts periodically, otherwise they may be discontinued. Many stores have different kinds of accounts. Most common will be the monthly account that you are expected to pay in full (although some stores will permit you to extend payments over a period and will charge you interest on the unpaid balance). Another type of account is the long-term arrangement for major purchases. Frequently, you will be asked to choose the length of payment period—12, 18, even 36 months. You then sign an agreement that you will pay for the purchase in equal installments plus interest.

Apply for an American Express card, Diners Club membership, or Carte Blanche card. They cost from $15 to $20 per year (fee may vary). Check out the benefits of each. American Express is the most popular of the three. BankAmericard and Master Charge don't charge fees to cardholders. It goes without saying that you should have these cards.

Many of these credit cards can be used to rent cars, as well as to take the place of the cash deposit customarily required when renting. They can also be used to pay for airline flights. (Credit cards are also offered by individual airlines for purchasing plane tickets.) You can get a charge card from a Bell System company that permits you to charge long-distance and toll calls to your home phone when you are away.

Be sure to check with the management of your organization to determine what credit cards or privileges are available to its employees.

These are useful and possible sources of credit. However, there may be restrictions applied to you. For example, you may find you do not at this time earn enough to qualify for certain cards or memberships. Your age may be a factor (some agencies will not rent cars to anyone under 25). If you are denied credit because you are a woman, you may be able to take legal action to force the credit to be extended.

How Do You Stand Financially?

What would you do if you got the "pink slip" tomorrow? Or, suppose you got an offer from another company in a different city—pay not so great but future opportunities unlimited. Could you afford to accept it?

Now is the time to start probing into your finances, with the counsel of a professional accountant or a friend who is well versed in financial matters, if possible. You may have more ready resources than you imagine, so take the time to think them through thoroughly.

1. How liquid are you? How much cash could you be sure of getting your hands on in an emergency? List your savings, securities, insurance cash values, readily salable assets such as a car, jewelry, antiques—everything that could be turned into cash in a couple of weeks.

2. What are your other sources of money? Could you refinance an outstanding loan or a mortgage? How easy would it be for you to borrow money—from family, a bank, a credit union?

Could you, if necessary, get an advance on money someone still living is leaving you in a will? Could you establish a plan now whereby you could someday borrow money without having to answer questions on employment at the time, such as getting a line of credit at your bank or an American Express Executive Money Card? Borrowing, of course, may not be sound fiscal policy, especially with interest rates high, but your survival might be at issue.

3. If you were fired, what kind of severance pay could you reasonably expect? Do you have part of a profit-sharing plan that can be withdrawn in cash?

In some states, receiving severance pay, no matter how large, has no effect on eligibility for unemployment compensation, which, incidentally, can be collected in a different city or state if the recipient is there looking for work. There is, however, one catch with severance pay: it is taxed as straight income. If the sum is large, the initial withholding tax can be limited to 25 percent—but the balance of the tax is due the following year.

Totaling your figures now will give you a pretty good idea of the liquid assets you could draw on. The picture you have may look rosier than you thought. But before you relax, you should look at your expenditures.

4. What are your inescapable monthly expenses—food, mortgage, rent, insurance payments, utilities, taxes, installment payments, and so on? These unavoidable costs almost always add up to more than you would expect them to be.

5. What new expenses would you have to add? If you can extend your benefits, such as health and medical insurance, you'll be picking up the whole tab now. And if you have to take out new coverage, premiums will be higher than they were under a group plan. If you intend to look for work in another city, you'll have extra costs for travel and lodging. Relocating also means a dent in the budget.

6. What expenses could you cut down? Convenience foods, snacks, luxury items, outside help, entertainment, liquor, clothes—the list is long.

7. What expenses could you cut out? Music lessons, club dues, contributions, and so forth.

8. What payments could be temporarily suspended? Lenders will sometimes agree to accept only interest payments for two or three

months if you can persuade them that your problem is only temporary. Life insurance premiums can often be paid by dipping into the policy loan value. You can let taxes slide for a while, if you file for an extension or notify the tax department, though you'll have to pay a penalty.

Now you know what it will cost you to keep going. How long will your liquid assets last? If the prospect looks gloomy or you are hesitant about exhausting all your resources, consider:

9. What could you do to bring in income, other than working in your own occupation? It may not be the job you had in mind, but money is money. And some people who are forced to take extra jobs end up liking them so well they never go back to their original field.

It is probably clear by now that periodic assessment of your financial status, using these questions as guidelines, can be a useful means of keeping your feet on the ground.

YOU

What kind of impression do you make? How do people react to you the first time they meet you or talk with you on the phone? Most of the time you get some feedback that indicates that they do or do not like you; and sometimes you can tell how much they like or dislike you. But only after you've known a person for some time do you find out if the image you project is the one you intend to project because you consider it most appropriate for your role, the relationship, and the circumstances.

How You Come Across to Others

Disregarding external factors for a moment, the impression you make depends largely on three things:

1. Your appearance—your physical attributes, how good-looking your face and figure are, whether your makeup and hair style are becoming, how attractive you are in motion (walking, gesturing), as well as in repose (sitting, standing), your clothes, whether they fit well and are the right style and color for you, and your overall image.

2. Your voice—how pleasant it sounds, its pitch and modulation, the degree to which it projects interest and enthusiasm, your language and vocabulary, your manner of speaking and the way you express yourself, and how effectively you communicate what you mean to say.

3. Your personality—the type of person you are, projected in part by your appearance and voice, but also by your behavior, how you conduct yourself in relationships, your attitudes and feelings about yourself and others, and the roles you assume.

Is Your Appearance an Asset?

Your figure. An attractive figure—that is, not being overweight or underweight—in addition to being better for your health, can help make a good first impression on interviewers when you're looking for a job and on the people with whom you deal in your organization. If you're too fat or too thin, by all means make a serious effort to change your eating habits.

If you need to lose weight, taking off 20 pounds can win you admirers, and taking off 50 pounds can change your life. Even if you find dieting difficult, don't rationalize about it; even thin people have to work at keeping thin. We know a woman whose heaviness caused her to be extremely anxious about her personal relationships, especially with men, and affected other people's attitudes toward her. She went on a diet, and by the time she had lost 50 pounds, her confidence and self-esteem had so improved that she applied for and got an executive position in a male-dominated organization. In fact, she was the first woman to hold the post.

Your face. Make the most of your features. Treat your complexion tenderly, by using lotions to protect it from the sun and wind (especially on the beach), by eating and drinking the right foods and beverages, and by getting enough rest. Use makeup that is kind to your skin. Shop around until you find a good line of cosmetics, possibly a reputable hypoallergenic variety. Seek advice from cosmetic salespersons about the best colors for your everyday makeup, making sure to keep it light and natural. If you like the look of the 30s—dark lipstick and nail polish—save it for evening.

If you're particularly displeased with your features—perhaps you don't like having crooked teeth or a large nose—you may want to consider seeing a specialist, such as an orthodontist or a plastic surgeon, to change the situation. However, your attitude is the most important element; if you and others like your face the way it is, it would be foolish to spend money needed for other things, as well as risking having something go wrong.

Your hair. Again the natural look is best. If possible, avoid having your hair set at beauty salons. Our mothers and grandmothers made weekly or biweekly trips to the beauty parlor, and they considered it a pleasant ritual. But if you intend to be a fast-track woman, you'll be better off if you free yourself from the hair spray necessary to maintain your hairdo between visits, the hours spent under the dryer, and the need to seek out hairdressers in unfamiliar cities when you're on trips.

Find an excellent hair stylist and ask him or her to help you select a convenient and attractive style and to teach you how to maintain it between haircuts. If you tint your hair, learn to do it yourself. A friend of ours decided to tally up what she was spending on her hair (for permanents, tints, washes, sets, cuts, and occasional oil treatments) and found it was $300 to $400 a year. She decided at that point to become a do-it-yourselfer and now spends $60 a year on her hair.

Your physical bearing. What is it that makes some persons stand out in a crowd, other than beauty? It's the way they walk, move, hold their bodies, stand, and conduct themselves; a quality of uniqueness or importance that they convey through their "body language." Some executive recruiters maintain that they can usually spot a man who earns a high salary and has an important job by the way he walks into a room.

Looking and acting as if you are a superior person can get you far, as young men breaking into highly competitive job markets can attest. Many of them are hired by large corporations more for what their appearances seem to reflect than for what is printed on their résumés. For young women, acquiring an air of importance, grace, poise, and polish can be very helpful.

Your wardrobe. Katherine Gibbs knew what she was doing when she insisted that the women who attended her secretarial course dress properly. So did the hundreds of secretaries who used to wear black pumps, and a black dress adorned by a single string of artificial pearls. In those days, you couldn't tell if a secretary came from a well-to-do family or a poor one.

Changing styles and attitudes have brought women greater choice in what they wear to work. Still, women should exercise care in choosing their clothes. Just because *Vogue* is showing flowing dresses with capped sleeves and the Palm Beach set is wearing embroidered jeans doesn't mean that these outfits are appropriate for the office.

In the interests of your career, it is best to stay with simple styles such as the tailored suit and the shirtdress. Mini and maxi lengths are to be avoided. Skirts should not be shorter than just above the knee and not longer than mid-calf; mid-knee length or just below the knee is best. Conservative pants suits are acceptable. Walking shoes and boots are also acceptable. In certain fields, such as advertising and publishing, clothing standards may be quite relaxed, and even blue jeans will be considered acceptable.

Because there is so much variety in style and quality of women's clothing, it is important that you be highly selective and purchase those items that are most suitable for your particular job and career situation. Here are some suggestions from women who moved out of nonstatus jobs into administrative or professional positions.

Build a basic wardrobe. First select your colors—a dark one (black, brown, navy), a light neutral (beige or gray), and one or more light to medium shades (blue, green, and so on)—and then buy your basic wardrobe in these colors. Basics include heavy and light coat, raincoat, several suits, several dresses, shoes, handbags, and gloves. For accessories such as blouses and scarves, and for additional dresses or separates, select pastels (yellow, pink, or blue if you're blond or brownette) or soft shades of medium colors (orange and red are good on brunettes) that harmonize with the darker wardrobe. And don't forget to add to your list a lightweight leather attaché case or other carrying case that will hold papers and books. An attaché case is not pretentious, and nothing looks worse than a well-dressed woman carrying a manila envelope or a shopping bag.

Buy clothes that are functional and multipurpose so your wardrobe will stretch further—a pants suit with matching skirt, a two-piece dress with matching jacket or sweater, or a suit with another color-coordinated skirt and blouse or vest. Try to buy clothing that is appropriate both in the evening and during the day and that can be worn three or four seasons of the year. Don't buy wool clothing in pastel shades, heavy winter suits that are too bulky to go under coats, white linens and piqués for the summer, all of which are appropriate in only one season and require drycleaning or ironing. It's also a good idea to stay away from most 100 percent linens and cottons, and from blouses and summer clothes that are labeled "Dry Clean Only."

Shop carefully and frugally. Your wardrobe is an investment that can help you gain entry to the kinds of jobs you want, so it's worth spending time shopping for it. But don't assume that your clothes have to be expensive. The difference in price is small between the less expensive items in the better stores and the more expensive ones in the moderate stores.

Stick with simple styles that are becoming and that are made of good fabrics. Keep an eye out for sales in the better stores and for discount stores whose clothes have labels in them or whose brands you can identify. One New Yorker, who routinely checks her favorite stores for sales, commented that the best bargains are those she simply runs across, not those announced in the newspaper.

Here are some suggestions from career women for making proper use of your wardrobe:

Dress in the morning as if you were dressing to go out in the evening. In this way you will be prepared if you wish to have lunch or dinner with a business acquaintance or if you unexpectedly have to attend an important meeting.

Dress slightly in advance of the season for important meetings, such as job interviews. For example, in late March wear a yellow or green flowered blouse or scarf, and in late August, camel color or brown. This generally creates a more favorable impression than clothing that typifies the season just ending.

Dress down, not up. If the lines of a dress or suit are good, but it has unessential frills, buttons, or bows, remove them. Get rid of brass buttons and substitute buttons that match the fabric. Avoid high fashion, and resist the temptation to buy "dressy" dresses. Keep purchases of current fashions to a minimum since they go out of style rapidly.

Enlist your boss's aid. If you are being groomed for better things, your boss is probably conscious of how you look to others. If no remarks about your clothes are forthcoming, ask for an opinion about a certain style or color (assuming the person has some taste) and whether he or she thinks it is suitable for the office (not whether your boss personally likes it, which puts the discussion on a different level).

Look at your wardrobe as an investment in the future. Obviously, it's not as important as your education, but it is an important factor when you are starting a career. You have to look right for the first interview to get invited back for the second, to get a job, and to be promoted to a better job. If you don't have the appearance of a potential manager, it may never occur to anyone but you and your boss that you are one.

Above all, buy and wear clothes that make you feel good. Within the framework of the conditions just discussed, your clothes should express the kind of person you hope you are (or soon will be), and they should make you feel attractive and add to your self-confidence. As pointed out by *Ms.* writer Tricia Kushner, the way we dress "projects an image of us to the outside world that affects how people respond to us, and it reflects an image inside which gives us a feeling about ourselves." [4]

How Do You Sound?

You've probably observed this dozens of times: You're attending a luncheon or cocktail party, and there's a beautiful woman everyone is ogling. People cluster around her and ask her for an opinion about the subject being discussed. She smiles and speaks—in a flat, dull monotone or in a high-pitched voice somewhat resembling that of a five-year-old child—and you immediately lose interest in her.

Without a doubt, one's voice and ability to communicate effectively with it are features overlooked by a majority of women. Their voices are too high, shrill, or sharp-edged, and they do nothing about it, even though many of them know how they sound. If you know or suspect that you have this problem, make a resolution to correct it right now.

When you make contact with someone on the telephone, a large part of the impression that person forms of you is based on your voice. Many jobs require a considerable amount of telephone work, often with persons who are important to the company but whom you've never met, such as customers, suppliers, purchasing agents, and executives inside and outside the company. Their reaction to you depends on the quality of your voice—whether it is vibrant and animated (which makes you sound interesting), as well as warm and relaxed (you're friendly and nice).

Your voice not only informs and persuades, but it expresses your feelings about yourself, other persons, the subject being discussed, and the overall situation. It can be an asset or a liability, because it can project self-assurance or insecurity, interest or indifference, happiness or depression.

Since your voice can indicate that you're out of control, you should learn to detect how you respond vocally to negative feelings, stress, adversity, and confrontation. Do you raise the pitch of your voice when you are nervous? Do you increase its volume when you're excited? When engaged in a face-to-face confrontation, do you talk too fast? If you have little awareness of how your voice gives you away, get some feedback from a friend or co-worker, so you can learn to control your responses.

Learn to speak up—or tone down—if you want to be heard. According to training specialists who work with young women in middle management jobs, one of the most common problems they have is that they don't seem to be able to determine the right volume to use when they speak to groups. Either they come on too strong and are too loud, or they are somewhat shy and too soft-spoken.

Even if you doubt that you'll ever have to give a speech to a large audience, you can benefit from a course in public speaking. Many colleges have adult education courses, as well as some YWCAs, at far less cost. If you don't want to take a course, you might buy or borrow a small tape or cassette recorder and practice speaking into it at home. Try out different vocal pitches, rhythms, volumes, and speeds, then concentrate on those that seem best for you. After that, check your articulation, intonation, and mannerisms. Make a list of the extraneous words that you use repeatedly, such as "you know" and "now"; of sounds that serve to fill up silences, such as "uh" and "ah"; and of favorite terms that you repeat too often. Use the tape recorder over and over until you are satisfied with the way you come across. Then if you do need to talk before a group, prepare your text or notes, and practice by speaking into the recorder.

You can get speaking experience by joining a local women's group and contributing to the discussions. Or you can become a member of another adult group (social, educational, or political) that meets regularly to discuss a topic that interests you, and join in the discussions. Better still, volunteer for special projects or tasks that require you to report back to the group.

There are books and study materials on speaking, written especially for women. Here are two that might interest you: Barbara Walters, *How to Talk with Practically Anybody About Practically Anything* (Doubleday, Garden City, N.Y., 1970, $5.95); and the Business and Professional Women's individual development plan, designed to help women develop their speaking ability and leadership potential. This is actually three courses of eight sessions each, costing only $1 per course, and may be obtained by writing to: Sales/Order Department, National Federation of Business and Professional Women's Clubs, Inc., 2012 Massachusetts Avenue, N.W., Washington, D.C. 20036.

Is Your Personality a Plus?

Personality per se is not discussed as much today as it was a few decades ago; instead we refer to behavior, traits, and personal characteristics. But psychologists still give personality tests designed to indicate to what extent a person is introverted or extroverted, dominant or submissive, self-sufficient or dependent, self-confident, sociable, and so on.

And, just as they did decades ago, many companies still hire certain types of people—traditionally men—to be groomed for executive positions, on the basis of the personalities that these people exhibited during their interviews or the results of the companies' assessment tests.

Although organizations frequently hire aggressive men, many react negatively to aggressive women. These organizations, or the men in them, like women to be soft-spoken and passive. Aggressive women make them feel threatened.

Given this situation, what can a woman with an aggressive personality do? She may choose to become more "feminine" in her behavior patterns, and to play more of the traditional feminine roles in her relationships with men. Even though it goes against the grain, this type of adjustment is not too difficult for most women. They can usually learn to accept it, at least for a while, once they realize it can help them get ahead. And some women even enjoy the challenge of assuming these roles in order to gain greater advantages.

Another approach that women can use to improve their relationships with men and women is the soft-sell, or public relations, technique, which combines femininity with selling skills. Career women need to learn how to convince others and win them over with sound arguments in a subtle way. One highly skilled saleswoman says that she combines these approaches by using her femininity during the early part of a sales call to give her time to determine what type of man she is calling on. If he is really traditional, she becomes more feminine; if he is contemporary, she reverts to her more professional, well-informed self.

As you read this chapter, you may have realized that you have your work cut out for you in developing your primary assets, or you may have felt that you're already well on your way in this area. In either case, we've provided you with many essentials that you'll need to begin (or continue) developing and using your assets to their best advantage.

REFERENCES

1. Douglas C. Basil, *Women in Management* (New York: Dunellen, 1972), pp. xi–xii.
2. John B. Parrish, "Women in Professional Training," *Monthly Labor Review,* May 1974, p. 421.
3. *Women's Work Has Just Begun.* Report on the Conference on the Redesigning of Work, The New School, New York, September 17, 1973.
4. Tricia Kushner, "Finding a Personal Style," *Ms.,* February 1974, p. 49.

5

CAREER
PATHS

A FRIEND who has a solid background in public relations commented recently that she wished she had made a career for herself instead of just holding down a series of jobs. "Considering how hard I've had to work, I really should have had a career," she said. "I'd be earning a decent salary instead of what I'm getting, and I'd probably be a manager by now."

She had developed good contacts in her field, plus excellent skills, and had held some positions that could have moved her up the promotional ladder. But she had always allowed her work to take second place to her personal life—her husband and his career, their daughter and her education, and their social life. Now she's in her mid-40s and she sees things from a different perspective.

YOUR CAREER

It is not that a woman might as well have a career; she should plan for and have one. Here are some rather convincing reasons:
• Every year the number of women who want to work, have to work, and do work increases.

• Many women are getting childbearing and child rearing out of the way sooner, working when their children are young, and then entering the job market at a younger age.

• More marriages are ending in divorce, and women can no longer count on receiving alimony from their ex-husbands.

• Women have become dissatisfied with traditional roles and relationships, in particular with marriage that confines them to the home, community, husband, children, and other housewives. They are overcoming their feelings of inferiority and ineptness and are no longer willing to be "put down" by men.

• Some wives are actively protesting by taking jobs, attending college or special courses, joining women's groups, and developing personal interests or a personal life that does not include their husbands, and a few wives are doing even more—they are leaving home to live alone and work, and experience their first taste of freedom.

Recent civil rights and equal employment opportunity laws have given women better salaries and more job and promotion opportunities. Technical and scientific developments have given women more freedom from housekeeping, cooking, and child-care chores. Unwanted pregnancy is less of a problem with effective methods of contraception and legalized abortion. Women are also experiencing greater acceptance by universities and colleges, business and industry, and even social groups.

Considering that you'll probably have to work during your lifetime, shouldn't you plan for it instead of going about it in a random manner, taking whatever jobs happen to be available when you need them?

You may be tempted to blame your husband for being nonsupportive and coercing you into staying at home, your boss for wanting you to stay in your present job, top-level executives in your company for policies and practices that keep you in a low-salaried "backroom" job, your father for not insisting that you attend a college of engineering or study for an MBA and for considering your brother's schooling and career plans more important than yours. However justified you may be, it's more important to start removing these obstacles than to blame people. To remove them, you may need to:

—Convince your husband of your career needs and of your desire to have his support. Be firm and don't back down if he objects.
—Talk with your boss so that he or she understands how you feel and is sold on the idea of helping you move ahead. If your boss balks and you're not likely to move up in your company, be prepared to leave—after you find a better job (unless your financial circumstances permit you to job-hunt at leisure).
—Develop outside contacts who will advise and inform you and help you find good job opportunities.
—Find out what skills and training are required for the occupations that interest you most—and go out and get them.

CHOOSING A CAREER PATH

The process of selecting a career is similar to other selection processes. You match your needs, preferences, and skills with what is available. In addition, you ascertain the occupations and fields you're best suited for right now, those you'd like to prepare to enter, the occupations and fields now open, and those that look most promising for the future.

There are many occupational factors that women should consider when they are selecting a career path.

Traditional Versus Nontraditional Occupations

Most jobs are sex-typed, that is, they involve activities that are considered natural for either men or women. For example, jobs that require physical stamina, aggressiveness, fearlessness, inventiveness, decisiveness, and leadership qualities are usually held by men. Jobs that involve detail, patience, and concern for people are generally reserved for women. Despite the fact that sex typing almost never has any rational basis, this practice continues to be employed.

The jobs traditionally held by women in this country are in the fields of teaching, nursing, and social work. It is no coincidence that they are an extension of the activities women perform in the home. To those we can add the jobs of waitress, seamstress, stewardess, secretary, bookkeeper, interviewer—none of which can provide a woman with a career unless she acquires enough resources and skills to become a restaurant owner, head of an apparel firm, airline executive, corporate secretary, partner in an accounting firm, or vice president in charge of personnel. However, this type of progress is rare because the fields are dominated by men. A woman who selects a nursing career is unlikely to become the chief administrator of a hospital; a female teacher has a slightly better chance of becoming a school principal; and a social worker has an even opportunity of being promoted to a director's position.

Women have a higher profile in retailing, publishing, public relations, and advertising. The traditional women's fields, especially teaching, don't offer a bright future for women just getting out of college, primarily because they are already flooded with women. Some of the traditional men's fields, such as sales and engineering, are much more promising. In fact, women with technical degrees are very much in demand today. And more promising still are those fields that are nontraditional or non-sex-typed, such as those relating to the computer sciences.

Profit Versus Nonprofit Organizations

Many traditional female occupations are found in nonprofit organizations—schools, foundations, hospitals, federal, state, and local government agencies and departments. The prevalence of women in teaching, nursing, and social work is well known; their presence and the degree of success that they have achieved in government and foundations is not so well known.

Government jobs provide considerable security, both remunerative and psychological. However, they carry less prestige than professional, academic, and business occupations. Also, their promotion paths are much more firmly defined and more elaborately structured, with a number of levels, on top of which sit appointees and 30- or 40-year men who can't be displaced. Therefore, it is the middle management jobs that women move into, and there they usually stay.

The one big plus of working for the government is that in order to obtain a job or a promotion the applicant must pass a standardized examination, such as a civil service exam. Applicants are then hired on the basis of their scores, thus giving women more opportunity to compete on an equal basis.

Professional Versus Nonprofessional Occupations

Professional occupations—doctor, lawyer, engineer, architect— are as highly esteemed as administrative and managerial occupations, hence have been the province of white, middle-class males. But they are also a preferred route of people from nonstatus groups who want to gain greater status and income.

Although the climb up the professional ladder is determined largely by knowledge and skills, the required special education is long and costly, the examinations are rigorous, and internship and certification by a band of professionals are difficult hurdles. Furthermore, once women win the appropriate degrees and certificates, they have a hard time getting into top-ranking hospitals, law firms, engineering consulting firms, architectural groups, and so on.

Although the welcome mat isn't really out for women to enter the professions and few of them aspire to professional status, if you have the desire, aptitude, stamina, tenacity, money, and time to become a professional accountant, architect, lawyer, psychologist, or doctor, the rewards will be great.

According to the Labor Department's *Occupational Outlook Handbook,* the fastest-growing occupational group over the next decade will be professional and technical positions that require a college degree. There will also be many service jobs available that require mechanical skills, such as repair of machinery, and service jobs (such as health care) that require training in technical schools or junior colleges plus apprenticeship on the job.

If you haven't yet selected a career specialty or are contemplating switching to another field, borrow or buy a copy of the *Handbook,* since it is a highly useful and informative book. The 1974–75 volume includes employment prospects for more than 30 major industries and 850 jobs. For each job there is a description of the nature of the work, training and education requirements, earnings, advancement opportunities, and geographic location of available jobs. You can purchase a copy of the current *Handbook* from a regional office of the Bureau of Labor Statistics, Department of Labor, or from the Superintendent of Documents, U.S. Government Printing Office, Washington, D.C. 20006. (Ask for BLS Bulletin No. 1785.) The price is $6.85, payable in advance, and the handbook is published biennially.

If you're seriously considering the professions (as well you should), the best place to go for information and assistance is the women's professional organizations. High on the list is the Society of Women Engineers in New York City (345 E. 47th Street), which has a Career Information Center and provides other types of help. For further details on this and other organizations, see the Resource List at the end of this book.

Organizational Versus Entrepreneurial Positions

Organizations in which you work as an employee should not just be viewed as "the employer." Contrary to the contentions of their critics, you are not just a subordinate to a superior, a willing or unwilling slave or victim of a system. Organizations are contexts in which you can learn and grow; they are groups of experienced people who are willing to pass their knowledge on to you, to demonstrate their skills so you can improve yours, and to give you an opportunity to try your wings in an environment that no one person could create. And the great advantage of this arrangement is that organizations will pay you to learn what your skills are, to learn how to perform new activities, and to find out how well you do in a variety of jobs. Furthermore, organizations provide you with a ladder to climb.

Despite the fact that organizations concentrate most of their training efforts on younger employees, age is no barrier to learning. You can devote decades to being a learner before you have to "rest on your laurels" and be content with job activities that merely repeat earlier experiences.

The other advantages, especially of larger organizations, are the benefits (among them, life insurance, medical coverage, disability insurance, pension programs) and the compensation system, which provides regular paychecks, salary reviews, and periodic increases. Yet some people believe that being in business for oneself is better—despite the longer hours, uncertainty about receiving steady income, and other disadvantages—because the person is her own boss.

The best course for a woman who wants to be self-employed is to work in an organization long enough to gain solid experience, and then to go into business for herself or freelance. In recent years more and more people have been seeking a second career that uses the expertise they gained in the first one.

For some persons, the decision about going into business for themselves is made easy by inheritance—the father has a business and wants to pass it on to the next generation. Another familiar route for women entrepreneurs is acquiring the business because their husband died and they are knowledgeable about it and dependent on it as a source of income for themselves and their children.

The traditional types of businesses established by women have been dress and hat shops, dry goods stores, restaurants, grocery stores (usually with their husbands), and interior decorating and real estate firms. Women will find other opportunities as a result of recent developments. As the demand for services has increased, different types of businesses and occupations have opened up that are tangential to both traditional male and female jobs—from the servicing of industrial machinery and consumer appliances to counseling and therapy.

Women will find when starting a business that their main problem is borrowing the capital necessary to finance the venture. The lending policies of banks have been notoriously discriminatory against women. Although the situation is changing, you are still likely to encounter difficulty—such as being required to have someone (usually your husband or father) co-sign the loan. Before attempting to borrow money, you should look into the lending policies of the banks in your area, find out about other possible sources of loans, and become well informed of your legal rights.

Generalizing Versus Specializing

As discussed in Chapter 4, a liberal arts degree will do little to help you find a career. A man who graduates from an Ivy League school with a liberal arts degree may be offered a job by a major corporation, but the chances of this happening to a woman are much smaller. Women will usually find they have to have better credentials and qualifications than men. Therefore, they fare much better if they acquire a specialty for which there is a demand in the job market. This is the surest path to a career.

Most in demand are these specialists: accountants, computer systems analysts, mathematicians and statisticians, engineers, and lawyers.

Those in moderate demand are chemists, economists, market researchers, and psychologists.

The low-demand fields, for which there are more qualified persons than there are jobs, should be avoided unless you are exceptionally talented—and strongly driven. These include the creative occupations—writing and editing; advertising copywriting and layout (artwork); television and film direction; photography for advertising, promotion, and public relations; and speech writing.

Don't succumb to the notion that specializing in "secretarial science" or office administration is a good tradeoff. The fields are already too full of women who are frustrated because they can't get promoted up or out, and whose salaries are too low. You can learn a lot and enjoy running an office or being administrative assistant to a president or vice president, but this isn't the stuff careers are made of. Most organizations just don't have routes upward from these positions.

Once you have established yourself as a specialist in an organization, you may find that organizational needs at certain levels emphasize general knowledge and experience rather than specialization. But most career paths lead out and up from a specialty.

Line Versus Staff Functions

Traditionally, organizations have two general types of functions—line, which are the functions most essential to the business, and staff, most of which are supportive or backup activities. In the typical consumer goods company, the most important line activity is selling, the second most important manufacturing, and most of the other activities are considered staff functions. In a bank, taking in and lending money are key line activities. In a consulting firm, providing consulting services is a chief line activity; in a manufacturing company, consulting is a staff function.

Generally, line functions are four-star avenues to the top. The salaries are higher, the prestige is greater, and the job activities are often those most essential to the route to the president's job.

Staff and service functions, such as advertising, promotion, and market research, are good avenues for women. Since women (even professionals) are usually given "backroom" or desk jobs, they can at least select a function that is important to the organization and therefore filled with top-notch, high-salaried executives who are likely to be promoted, that has interesting staff and service jobs that women may obtain, and that occasionally presents opportunities for women to advance into key jobs usually held by men. Although still somewhat rare, the frequency with which women in marketing staff and service jobs are being promoted to selling positions is increasing.

For women who much prefer dealing with dollars and cents instead of customers and markets, there is another excellent avenue— accounting and finance. Becoming a certified public accountant requires less education than many other professions and the field is considerably more versatile than many others. It also provides good compensation. Unlike specialists in marketing, which is strongly tied to specific industries, accountants and financial specialists are able to move easily from consumer goods firms to industrial products companies, from corporations to public accounting firms, from profit-making corporations to nonprofit organizations, and from small companies to large ones.

While staff positions may not offer career paths upward, the knowledge and experience that can be gained in some staff jobs can contribute substantially to your growth. You should therefore consider making lateral moves between line and staff jobs when it seems advantageous for you to do so. Following are some of the factors you should consider in making your choice.

If you've only had one job in one company in one industry, you would probably be surprised to learn of the many differences in operation, climate, and resources that exist from company to company in the same industry, from industry to industry, and from city to city.

Type of Industry

This country has gone through several stages in its business growth. The early stages centered on basic production, namely, agriculture, mining, and forestry; the later ones on primary industry, such as metal processing and manufacturing. These fields have remained male strongholds, as have the areas of railroads, utilities, insurance, and finance. Other industries that have effectively screened out women are construction, dockwork, warehousing, and trucking.

Before selecting a particular field or industry for beginning your career, consider the important factor that some areas offer more mobility than others, especially if you are in certain types of jobs. For example, in the airline industry, reservation agents and sales managers who want to make a move do not have many choices open to them. They can go with another airline, another transportation company, a travel agency, or a hotel. Other industries not easy to switch out of are utilities, insurance, retailing, and banking. Similarly, foundations and other nonprofit organizations and the education field can be difficult to leave after one has been in them for a number of years.

However—and this is an important qualifier—the extent to which you get locked into a particular industry depends on the type of job you have. The more closely related it is to the industry, the less freedom you have. As has already been pointed out, selling is very market-related, just as manufacturing is extremely process-related. Engineering also ties one to specific processes and sometimes to specific materials. But the boundaries of accounting, finance, computer services, and personnel, which involve dollars, data, and people, are usually easy to cross. By all means, check with people who are knowledgeable about the characteristics of a specific field or industry before you commit yourself to a long-term job or career in it.

Size of Company

The importance of size is that, in general, the larger the company the more likely it is to have job specifications and job descriptions, definite salary ranges for each job, a formal selection and hiring procedure, regular performance and salary reviews, training and management development programs, manpower planning that enables it to spot high-potential people, additional job opportunities and career paths, an EEO coordinator, and a variety of other invaluable resources, such as a library stocked with magazines and books on management, directories that contain information on companies (useful for job hunting), co-workers, managers, and others who have worked elsewhere and whose knowledge and contacts may be helpful to you. Above all, women will find a variety of staff and service jobs in large companies.

A recent trend observed among young male MBA graduates is their greater preference for small and medium-sized firms. They seem to feel that small firms offer greater opportunity for broader and more varied managerial and entrepreneurial experience; that it's more difficult to move up in large corporations; and that large corporations are less ethical and honest than small firms because they exploit their power. But some employment specialists say they detect greater interest in large companies on the part of MBAs, probably as a result of the current recession.

It is true that women who work in small firms receive many opportunities, and sometimes even get preferential treatment—if their bosses like them and think they can handle more responsibility.

But frequently jobs in small companies require more negotiation and taking initiative (for things such as salary increases and promotions that are built into the policies and practices of large companies), and career women, who already have enough obstacles to contend with, may not want to add these others. In view of this, a woman might want to look for a company, large or small, that has an affirmative action program, which provides some guarantees that she will not be discriminated against.

Another factor to consider is how much risk you're willing to take. Large, glamorous industries are known for their impersonal personnel practices. Among those that lay off individuals, groups, and even entire departments or divisions without hesitation are advertising, consulting, publishing, and television. Another high-risk industry is aerospace, not so much because it is glamorous but because it is highly dependent on government contracts. However, in this case the risk is somewhat offset by higher starting salaries than those in many other industries.

You should also consider how the industry holds up during a recession. The glamour fields get very shaky; their employees are among the first to feel the bite when companies cut expenses by eliminating unnecessary services.

Location of Industry and Company

Where the industry is situated can also be an important factor. Some industries are clustered in one or two areas. For example, aerospace is in California; electronics and research and development are also in California and near Boston; textiles are on the East Coast, especially the southern states; and, of course, the automotive industry is in the Midwest.

Most advertising, consulting, publishing, radio and television, and the garment trade (apparel design) are concentrated in New York City. The headquarters of many large corporations are clustered in the New York City area. Yet many of the employees of these companies probably work in offices and other facilities located elsewhere.

Location or, more precisely, relocation seems to be one of the biggest hurdles for women to overcome. When they are in their early 20s, many of them hesitate to move to a larger city unless they have relatives or friends in the area, or some of their college friends move there with them. Working wives with children are even more reluctant, unless they are career women earning high salaries or holding prestigious positions such as government official, college president, or head of an advertising agency.

Women in their 30s and 40s with established careers, dependents, and no husbands to help support the family are generally the most willing to relocate.

If you have never had the experience of living or working in a small town, and you are considering a job in one, think it through. Small-town living has lots of pluses, but privacy isn't among them. Regardless of what people say, they'll judge you on the basis of what you do after work as well as during work. So unless you live a fairly reserved life and enjoy participating in, or at least are willing to adjust to, small-town activities, you probably shouldn't make the move. On the other hand, if you are tired of the fast pace and congestion of a big city, you might find small-town living a welcome change.

If you work in a large city, you can job-hunt while you are employed and switch jobs without relocating. A large city also offers an array of valuable resources, such as employment agencies, counseling services, women's groups, colleges and universities, special courses, libraries, and stores.

Climate of Company

Almost nothing is more important than the style and quality of management in a company. Unless management is democratic and committed to providing equal opportunity, you won't find the climate conducive to your receiving the responsibility, promotions, and salary increases you deserve.

Before taking a job with a particular company, find out about their management policies. If their executives are old-fashioned and authoritarian or if they treat you with excessive chivalry, you may be dealing with a company that is not about to give up its stereotyped attitudes toward women.

However, there are many old-fashioned, paternalistic companies that are recent converts to the working woman's cause. In them you will get all the opportunity you could hope for. Quite a few paternalistic companies are leaders in their industries, and they pride themselves on their democratic personnel policies—which they really do practice. Very often they pay above-average salaries, have excellent benefits, and are a far better risk than companies that seem to be more modern. Some of these "modern" firms offer lower starting salaries and poorer benefits and are far less interested in the well-being of their employees. In fact, you should beware of companies that pay below-average salaries to men in lower-management echelons, especially if they are actively competing for high-salaried, top-level jobs. These men can harbor much hostility and resentment toward women who join their ranks.

In summary, the factors that must be considered in choosing a career path are many and varied. And since they have long-range implications for your career success, they should all be carefully weighed before you undertake the specifics of job hunting.

6

JOB HUNTING

IF you were asked to name some of the most traumatic events you had ever experienced, what would you reply? An accident? An operation? Moving to a strange city? Getting fired? For many of us job hunting would be one of those events, especially if it occurred when we were fresh out of college, in a strange city, or had just been fired or "laid off."

Job hunting is an experience that can shake the foundations of your self-confidence, unglue your ego, and make you wonder what on earth ever made you believe you were intelligent and capable to begin with. And one of the things that makes it so difficult—in addition to lack of money—is that friends and acquaintances will try to advise you by relating their own disheartening experiences. And though a few of them may give you some good tips, they can't help you sort through your feelings. That you have to do yourself.

Many people react to job hunting as if it's something to be endured, like a session in the dentist's chair. And if you've ever had a traumatic experience in either, you know one thing: it doesn't always get easier with practice. Ask a $60,000-a-year vice president who suddenly finds himself looking for another position. The older you get and the more responsible your job, the harder the experience can hit you.

We talked with women who had been forced to job-hunt in recent years because of cutbacks and layoffs in their companies. Here are some of the things they said about being caught in the purge:

> There wasn't much I could do. Jack [who held the other staff job like hers] hadn't been with the company as long as I had, and his skills weren't as good as mine, but after all, he's a man. [So was their boss.]

> I should have left long ago. I saw what was happening, realized it could affect my job; in fact, underneath I sensed it would affect me. But for some reason I just sat there and did nothing. [When this woman was laid off, her job functions were taken over by a man with no previous experience at that type of work.]

> We all knew about the cutbacks in the budget and production, but none of us thought it would happen so quickly. My résumé was up to date, and the timing was okay for me. But I hadn't really figured out what directions I should or could move in. [This woman was let go during the first wave of firing, even though as a manager she earned less and did more than three of the male managers who were retained for another six weeks, until the company folded.]

All three women went through a period of unemployment—the first one, three months; the second, seven months; the third, just three weeks.

Let's sum up the primary causes of hurried job hunting plus some other factors that can put you in a job bind:

—Not keeping your eyes and ears open to detect changes in your industry, your company, or your boss's attitude.
—Not following developments occurring in your own job market.
—Not establishing and maintaining good job-hunting resources,

or staying in touch with agencies or recruiting firms that could have kept a weather eye open for another job.

—Forgetting that being capable on the job isn't a guarantee that you'll keep it.

—Not having an updated résumé or a portfolio of your work.

—Not being mentally prepared for making a job change, let alone for job hunting.

—Not talking with your boss or your boss's boss or any other executive about being a reference for you.

—Not trying to negotiate with your boss or your boss's supervisor about doing freelance or part-time work, or using an empty office while you're job-hunting.

In short, if you are upset and unprepared, you will assume a defensive role instead of an offensive one. Women are far more likely to find themselves in this situation than men because women tend to have subordinate positions, regardless of their titles. Because the assumption is that they will remain in subordinate positions, they simply get pushed out of the way.

Since the business world and the men who occupy it can only be expected to change slowly, the major changes will have to be made in yourself. That is the purpose of this book—to help you develop more insights and broader perspectives, in addition to providing you with tools and techniques and sources and resources that will move you ahead faster and further up the corporate ladder, if not in the company where you now work, then in another company where your capabilities will receive more recognition.

This chapter will provide you with a rapid rundown of the basic tools and techniques needed for effective job hunting. It does not exhaust the subject. However, there are numerous books, pamphlets, and articles available from the government, universities, women's organizations, recruiting firms, publishers, and other groups; so if you need more information, you'll have no trouble obtaining it. And in the Resource List at the end of this book you will find the names of many organizations and the titles of some of the better books, to make sure you get off to a good start in mapping out your career campaign.

CHANGING JOBS

Knowing how and when to change jobs is one of the most difficult aspects of career building. Actually, the best time to start planning to leave a job is *before* you become aware of a strong motivation or need to do so. Often a woman will experience a period of ambivalence and vacillation: she enjoys the job one day, agonizes over it the next. One day she feels she can't stand another eight hours of it, but by the next day she has persuaded herself that she should stay. If you are experiencing these feelings, it is time to update your résumé, check the job market, and start drawing up a job-hunting plan.

Here are other conditions that should prompt you to prepare for a job change:

You don't like your job. The work has become monotonous. You suffer from job fatigue, are bored, and are sometimes indifferent about the quality of your work. You hate Mondays—and every other weekday. You take an increasing amount of time off for personal reasons. You realize you are only staying there because of the security the job provides.

The job isn't big enough, and there's no opportunity for advancement. You don't have as much responsibility or as many activities as you were led to expect (or as once satisfied you). The job is narrow and unchallenging, making little use of your knowledge and skills. You've tried to find ways to expand it, but now you can't anymore without encroaching on someone else's territory. And your boss can't, or won't, find other work for you.

Or, you have a great job (or at least you've had a great job), you like your boss and the company, the pay is good, but you've been doing the same thing for five years. You're fairly happy with the setup but no longer very stimulated. The positions that you might logically be promoted to are filled and will remain that way for some time. And when someone leaves, you feel that you will not be seriously considered as a replacement.

Your salary is too low. You know that the men in your organization—and women in similar jobs in other organizations—earn more than you do. When you try to discuss your salary situation with your boss or with personnel, you get shrugs or vague talk about what a tough year it is or hints that perhaps next year you'll get the raise you've been asking for.

You don't like your boss. The longer you know him, the more aware you become that he is intolerant, authoritarian, unjustly demanding. He treats all women as if they were his inferiors. He may be a petty, self-serving dictator or a chauvinist who sees women only as sex objects.

The status of your boss has changed. He or she may have been downgraded in relative importance in the organization. Some responsibilities may have been taken away (and given to someone else). Or to put it bluntly, you may be standing behind a loser. Even worse, you suspect that when your boss leaves, his (or her) job will be phased out or merged with another, leaving you nowhere.

The organization is growing alien to you. Management movement has slowed or is static. The old ways prevail. Or it seems as if nothing is really happening, and everyone is drifting. There is little interest in developing new managers—or improving the skills of the old ones. The organization seems little concerned with the welfare and interests of its key people. Secrecy and faulty communications prevail. You witness favoritism, arbitrariness in decisions, procrastination in recognizing and solving problems. There are rumors of infighting at the top and evidence of no more than grudging cooperation between peers.

In addition to these situations, there are other symptoms, but they all say essentially the same thing: it's time to change jobs. The woman who is building a career cannot afford to stay very long in the kinds of job situations we've described here. It is not an exaggeration to say that the upwardly mobile woman, from her first day on the job, must develop her resources in preparation for her next move—which may come sooner than she expects.

DEVELOPING A JOB-HUNTING STRATEGY

Is it possible to avoid being caught in a layoff and being faced with the sudden need to job-hunt? Not completely, but there are certain steps you can take that will minimize the chances.

A few years ago, our first suggestion would have been that you become very knowledgeable about business and the job market. However, with today's murky employment picture, we recommend instead that you first consider the reasons for remaining in your present job, taking a different job in the same company, or moving to another company.

The first step in developing a job-hunting strategy is to learn to recognize risk situations. Look for risks *before* you get into them, so you can determine whether they're worth taking. Risks occur in a variety of situations, conditions, and places—certain industries and companies, specific jobs and occupations, particular types of bosses or company management, and job relationships. Any one or a combination of these factors can put you in an insecure position.

We have already mentioned some of the high-risk fields, such as advertising, publishing, and consulting, where layoffs are common, especially during recessions; and government-funded aerospace and defense-product industries, in which the loss of a contract can put thousands of employees out of work.

There are also certain types of companies in which employees have little job security. Among these are newly formed companies that may be adversely affected by a sudden swing in economic conditions; new companies in industries that have a high mortality rate; subsidiaries recently acquired by larger corporations that want to reorganize and eliminate excess staff; companies that have a high turnover of upper-level executives or in which all of top management has recently been replaced. In addition, a particular firm can be a risky place to work because its profits and sales have been down the past few years due to poor management decisions or because its volume of business has been cut back due to shortages of materials or hard times in the industry.

There are also high-risk jobs, such as new positions created for handling functions not yet generally accepted by the company executives, some token positions given to women so the company can comply with the Office of Equal Employment Opportunity, and certain "control" jobs in computer and auditing work.

Frequently a job is risky because of one incompetent or overambitious executive. He or she may be your immediate supervisor, the head of the department or division, or even the head of the company. The further up the ladder this person is, the greater his or her effect on the organization.

There are also some low-risk, highly stable organizations—such as government agencies, utilities, banks, insurance companies, and firms in government-regulated industries—where you're unlikely ever to be fired unless you're highly inefficient or impossible to get along with.

Even if your job seems to be risk-free, remember that there is some degree of risk in every position. The executive who seemed charming and talked of the job enthusiastically during the initial interview can turn out to be an authoritarian who really only wanted a secretary or an assistant to handle routine tasks. The boss with whom you had a great relationship, who gave you excellent training and promotions, can, on being given added responsibility, turn into a dictator.

Keep your eyes and ears open for signs that indicate you've gone about as far as you can go, such as a change in the way your boss treats you or comments that he makes about you to others. (The comments may be made in front of you or may get back to you via others.) You'll have to be the judge of whether you can discuss the problem with your boss. If you do try to get your boss to level with you, and he or she feigns innocence or is hostile, you will have just compounded your problem—and probably increased the chances that you'll soon be out job-hunting.

When you hear rumors about future changes in your department or company, the new boss you're getting, or a new employee who will be doing the same work as you, make a real effort to find out more about the change. Then decide if and when you should start preparing to leave. Is it better to wait until the purge comes and you're asked to leave, on the assumption that your boss and others will help you find a new job? Even if you don't find a new job before you're laid off, we suggest that you start your job-hunting campaign while you're still employed. Your bargaining powers with a prospective employer are certainly better if you're in a less desperate situation, and if you lose your present job before you find a new one, you'll have the advantage of already having a well-developed job-hunting plan. It will also help you collect unemployment insurance during this time, since you'll have to register with your state employment service and provide evidence that you're looking for a job.

On the other side of the risk situation, if you have some money in the bank, lots of ambition, and the stamina of a risk-taker, you can take a promising job in a fast-moving company. Then, if it doesn't work out, you can resign before you've been there long enough for it to even appear on your résumé.

Whether your tolerance for risk is large or small and your present job secure or insecure, be realistic about your current situation and your future. After all, there are fewer reasons than ever for working women to stay submerged in subordinate positions, so you shouldn't hesitate to carefully examine your job situation. The worst thing that can happen is you'll find you don't actually like it.

The second step in your job-hunting strategy is to be well informed about business, industries, and companies—especially your own. You should read the business section of your local newspaper plus several other national business papers and magazines regularly. The top general publications are *The Wall Street Journal* and *Business Week*. These will keep you advised about the state of the economy and recent business developments. But since they provide only occasional articles about specific industries and companies, you should also read some trade journals, which provide news and information about your occupational field and about your industry.

Learn all you can about your own company by studying the annual report, reports and memos from top management, and company newsletters. If you can't find much information, and the company has no library, ask your boss if he or she has any materials (not confidential ones, of course) that you might read to get a better idea about the company. If your boss is willing to give you some briefing sessions, you might also induce him (or her) to explain the annual report, tell you about the competition, describe the markets and customers, production process, and so on. And, while you're talking about it, get your boss to recommend a few management books that will be helpful to you.

Before you go for a job interview, get some information about the company. You can ask one of your acquaintances who works there or contact a local business library to find out the company's products, sales volume, earnings, number of employees, name and title of the executive who heads one or more of the departments. Some business libraries will give you this data over the phone.

If during your interview you are told you'll be asked to return to talk with other persons, you might then request information about the company. (This indicates that *you're* interested.) If you're provided with only a personnel booklet that explains such things as the company's vacation policy and benefits, ask for an annual report. If none is available, after you leave, telephone the company's public relations department or treasurer's office—or have a friend call for you if the firm is small—and request an annual report. (If the firm is privately owned, it may not have an annual report available to the public.).

Familiarize yourself with the various business directories, such as those published by Dun & Bradstreet and Standard & Poors. If your local library doesn't have them, try the university libraries, or even those of large companies in your area. Business directories are not only useful for reference, they are just what you need to develop your own mailing list for a direct mail job-hunting campaign. The directories are too expensive for the individual to buy, so they have to be used in the library, but there are special reports or issues of magazines that cost only a few dollars and can be used for general reference or in conjunction with the directories, such as *Dun's* magazine's annual issue that provides a summary of the previous year's developments in each major industry, and *Fortune* magazine's listing of the top 500 industrial companies plus the top 50 firms in finance, insurance, merchandising, transportation, and utilities.

The third step is to know the job market and the conditions within your occupation or profession. Subscribe to the best publications available—newsletters, magazines, journals, employment listings—that provide current information about trends in your field, the availability of jobs, and salaries being paid. If there are no publications of this sort in your field, find out if there is a professional or business association that collects salary information, maintains lists of persons seeking employment, or provides other types of assistance. (Some associations conduct periodic salary surveys.)

A number of women's groups (see the Resource List at the end of this book) have formed within some of the professional associations. These are better geared and more highly motivated to help women who are seeking jobs and who want to further their professional careers than are the other associations, whose membership and administration are predominantly male. By belonging to one of these women's groups through membership in their association, you'll automatically receive publications and be able to establish contacts. And even if you don't belong, by expressing interest in becoming a professional, you'll find that a number of the association staff members and elected officers will be most helpful to you.

You should be thoroughly familiar not only with your occupation or profession but with related areas that interest you or that you have some qualifications for. Beginning with entry-level jobs, you should know what the jobs involve (responsibilities, types of activities, skills); their salary; what organizations have these jobs; how far up the ladder one can go and by what routes; at what points women are usually blocked and what other options they have; and, especially, how much and what type of education are required for the job at various levels.

The fourth step in your job-hunting strategy is to get a clear idea of where you stand, where you want to go, and how you're going to get there. Find out where you stand in the company in which you work—what your status is, was, or may be in the future, and how your salary ranks compared to other persons in similar jobs. Make an effort to learn the salary ranges for the different job classifications. This information is often more easily obtained when you are being interviewed by a company than when you're already employed there, since personnel managers are less likely to consider salary ranges and structure confidential than are departments heads.

How can you find out what your co-workers are making? Do a bit of socializing. Go out to lunch with a well-informed, talkative co-worker, or have a couple of drinks with him or her, either during lunch or after work. Chat over drinks or a meal with a fellow employee who has recently been fired or laid off, or who resigned in a huff because of a falling out with a boss or disgruntlement about lack of promotion or salary increase. You can learn a lot this way.

After you get a fairly realistic idea of where you stand in your own company, try to determine where you stand in the job market. Would it be difficult for you to get a better job—or even a comparable one—in another company? If so, why? Were you moved into a position of responsibility because your boss had confidence in your abilities, even though you lacked the experience, skills, or education usually required for the job? Or do you have the reverse situation, in which your education, skills, and previous experience far exceed the requirements of the job? In either case, have you decided to stay in the field or do you want to leave it, and are you already angling for a job in a field where you'll be able to put your talents to better use?

Whether you aspire to a higher-ranking job in your company or a better job elsewhere, you've got to have the appropriate credentials. So when you compare yourself to others, you have to look at more than job responsibility, title, and salary. In addition to previous experience, what specific education and training do the fast-track persons have? And, considering today's tight employment situation, what kind of credentials do you need to ensure that you'll get into, stay, and move upward in your chosen field, and in other fields that interest *you?* Be honest with yourself about this. Many women tend to underemphasize or overemphasize the importance of a professional education—especially if they're the ones who made it to the top via the secretarial route without a college education or the ones who have just gotten their doctorates and are making as much as many women managers who have worked for 20 years. As we've said before, a degree in liberal arts will not get you nearly as far in your chosen field as will a specialized education. So, by all means, do whatever you can to acquire the credentials needed for the field you want to enter.

Once you set your sights on specific goals, you can save yourself considerable anxiety and possible grief if you also establish secondary goals and draw up alternate plans. First you have to evaluate career paths: list the various job possibilities, beginning with entry-level positions, and the different routes in the types of organizations in which you want to work; list the educational, skill, and experience requirements for each position; then list the requirements for working in other types of organizations. What salaries do they pay? How easily can you move from one type of organization to another? What special requirements are part of the job—such as relocation, travel, commuting? What special advantages does a company offer—such as company-paid education, excellent benefits, job security? Then draw up a chart on second and third career possibilities, assuming they interest you almost as much.

Now consider two essentials: time and money. How long will it take you to get the extra qualifications? (Specify a minimum and a maximum time.) How long should you stay in an average-to-good job that offers little potential? Do you have skills for which there is a ready market in case you need to take on an extra job or you suddenly find yourself unemployed—even to do temporary office work, if necessary? Those extra skills can provide you with a secondary or even a tertiary line of defense during a recession, or if you opt to return to college and need to make some money.

PREPARING YOUR RÉSUMÉ

Always keep your résumé up to date, instead of revising it only when you're looking for a new job. In this way, you'll be spared the annoyance of having to update it in a hurry when you're job-hunting. And you will be able to review your progress and the direction your career is taking as you move into new jobs or add new responsibilities. You'll also be prepared if an organization to which you belong asks you for a *curriculum vitae*.

There is no one type of résumé that is best for all kinds of people and jobs. But there are certain basic principles that can guide you in producing a highly readable and impressive record of your experience and education.*

* An example of a completed résumé may be obtained free from Cris Associates, 274 Madison Avenue, New York, N.Y. 10016; a form for a résumé may be obtained free from Catalyst, 6 East 82nd Street, New York, N.Y. 10028. Cris Associates can also send you a checklist on what to do in an interview, and Catalyst can provide you with addresses of counseling and placement centers.

Brevity. A one-page résumé is definitely preferable, especially early in your career. It should be carefully written to detail the important facts about yourself. Later in your career you can expand it to two pages, but it isn't recommended that you enlarge your résumé beyond that. It is undoubtedly more desirable to make the résumé attractive and readable than to cram in every detail. If you're in a field where a prospective employer might want to see samples of your work, keep an up-to-date portfolio or notebook that you can offer to show later. This portfolio might include examples of artwork, copywriting, reports, forms designed, brief descriptions of major projects, and so on.

Responsibilities and results. What you have *done* is most important. After the title, company name, and location, describe fully and realistically your responsibilities and the results you achieved. For example: "Responsible for drafting new policies and developing new procedures to improve response to customer inquiries. These new procedures were largely responsible for increasing the percentage of same-day responses from 68 percent to 86 percent."

And while you're reviewing your responsibilities, check to see how many you perform in your boss's name that he might give you permission to take credit for. Also, if your boss has an impressive title, state it in the job description: "Reported to the vice president, marketing."

Priority and recency. Your current or most recent job should appear first, and this merits the most information. Some résumé writers give equal weight to everything they've done, with the result that the résumé is hard to digest and too much of the less important data is remembered afterward by the reader. Besides, the experience, skills, and knowledge that you acquired years ago depreciate rapidly in this fast-changing world unless you have continued to use them in your more recent jobs.

Should you include part-time work? Yes, especially if there have been significant gaps in your full-time employment history, or if the part-time work has been relevant to your career progress. And that's particularly true of work done during school years, if you're a recent graduate.

Education. Generally this information should follow employment history. In addition to business school or university, your major field, and degrees (and when they were conferred), be sure to include continuing education (such as night classes) and specialized training.

Personal data. Many people omit birth date or age (and it's illegal for employers to ask) and state of health. Some exclude marital status and number of dependents. Your name, address, and telephone number should, of course, be prominently displayed at the top for easy reference. Personal interests such as tennis, skiing, and writing poetry are not usually considered important. It may be worthwhile to mention membership and activities in clubs and professional associations, or community involvement as a volunteer or elected official, so this information should follow education history.

Young persons with little job history should include details about school, college, and club activities; scholarships and awards; and interests. This gives the reader a more complete picture, and provides a slightly longer résumé.

References. Neither employment nor personal references should be included on your résumé. You probably will not want your present company or boss contacted until you're certain you're leaving. Therefore, protect yourself by telling the interviewer that no references are to be contacted until that time or without your knowledge. Most companies will want to check your present or previous employers, after which they may contact your college and even run a credit check on you. (This is standard procedure.)

Salary. Don't put the salary you want on the résumé. In job-hunting you are often in a position to negotiate, so don't commit yourself to a figure before you really have to. If you're applying for a job by mail, your salary requirements should be stated in the covering letter.

Also, do not put your current salary on your résumé. If your present company has been underpaying you, you don't want to give the new company any ideas that it can too. In addition, if you have a responsible job but a low salary, the interviewer may think that you have inflated the description of your job to make your position seem more important than it actually is. The point is that you want to sell *yourself* to the company before you give information, such as a low salary, that may put you into a "slot" below your capabilities and experience and below the position for which you're applying.

Other omissions and inclusions. If you've had one or two brief stints in low-level jobs that didn't work out well, by all means omit them. They do nothing to help your cause, and they just clutter up the page. If, however, they were interesting or unusual jobs, and if you can get good references from the persons you worked for, you should include them.

If you lack job experience, it is especially important to include short-term jobs as well as other kinds of paying and nonpaying activities, such as being a camp counselor, tutor, hospital volunteer, or an officer in the local chapter of a well-known organization. But as you gain work experience, you should drop a number of these items from your résumé.

Some persons include a statement of career objectives—and some employment specialists encourage this. However, it tends to restrict the use of your résumé, and you don't want to close off any possibilities.

Exaggeration. Many résumé writers succumb to the temptation to exaggerate their abilities, education, and experience, or to take credit for something they haven't done. Professional recruiters say that they can detect this easily because the person looks too ideal. Exaggerations usually become evident when employers, schools, and other references are contacted. This can haunt applicants for years, and outright distortions or falsehoods can cripple a career permanently.

Your résumé should be rewritten every time you have a major job change. However, if you've been moved out of a job you like into one you don't like, and an opportunity comes along that will put you back in the preferred job function, by all means use the old résumé, with the excuse that you haven't been actively job-hunting. This is a good tactic in many job-hunting situations, since a happily employed person has a higher market value than a malcontented one.

Make sure your résumé is attractive and easy to read, that the most important facts can be grasped quickly even by a casual reader, and that the patterns and continuity of your career are apparent. Remember, you're not trying to supply a definitive autobiography. You want to spark enough interest to make someone reach for a telephone.

How to determine your compensation. There have been some breakthroughs for women in the area of compensation since the Equal Pay Act was passed in 1963. Once women began discovering that they were legally entitled to earn as much as men for doing the same type of work, they increasingly resorted to those means available under law and regulations to achieve actual equality. As a result of these actions by women, the courts are now awarding back compensation in cases where there has been inequity and are forcing business organizations to change salary and job classifications to bring men's and women's compensations into line with each other.

But progress in lifting women's earnings to the levels enjoyed by men has been—and probably will continue to be—slow. According to a study based on U.S. Census data, in 1970 female operative and service workers earned 50 percent of what male workers in those categories did, and female professional and technical employees weren't much better off: they earned slightly less than two-thirds of what men in their classifications did. Even in equivalent clerical jobs, women were paid only 79 percent of men's average weekly earnings.[1]

The disconcerting evidence today is that these gaps are growing, not diminishing. The point for you is that in looking for a job, you cannot automatically assume that you will not continue to be disadvantaged as a woman. And because your initial salary is a large determinant of how much you can earn while in the organization, you need to get as many facts as possible about what salaries are paid for specific jobs in certain companies and industries. (These salaries can differ widely from area to area.) As you may already have found out if you've been working, salary information is often hard to come by, even in your own company.

Here are some suggested ways you can collect compensation data. They may not always produce the exact information and precise figures you'd like, but they can be used to develop ranges and guidelines to help you negotiate an equitable salary.

1. Interviews with corporations, employment agencies, and

search firms can give you some clues to ranges for particular jobs in an industry. Women often don't take advantage of such interviews to gain such general knowledge. You should view them as opportunities not only to discuss a particular position but to acquire comparative data that will help you to comfortably and confidently establish your own salary expectations.

2. Read classified and display ads in newspapers and in trade, professional, and industry journals. You can find some compensation data in women's publications and government publications. Also, various business and professional organizations conduct compensation surveys. Much of this kind of material can be found in business libraries: Your present firm may have its own, or a large public library may have a business section. The *Business Periodicals Index* will direct you to articles on compensation.

3. Ask friends, acquaintances, and relatives. If you are uncomfortable asking people to give you salary information directly, preface your request with the explanation that you are considering possible career paths for yourself. Also, pick the time and place so that your potential informant is relaxed and less likely to think you are simply pumping. Incidentally, you'll probably find that men are more likely to give you specifics than women, either because they're earning more money or because they find a woman's questions less threatening to them.

There may be some job interviews in which you're reluctant to force the salary issue—especially in the early, exploratory phase of an interview. But as soon as it appears that you and the company have a mutual interest, find out the salary range for the job (minimum and maximum) as well as what the company reasonably anticipates paying a new employee who has the requisite skills, education, and experience. In subsequent discussions, assuming their interest has grown to the point of hiring, you can get more details. For example:

—How will the size of the salary increases be determined? Will they be 5 percent a year, 10 percent? What are the criteria for an increase?

—What kinds of pay increases would be attached to a promotion? Are such increases open and unrestricted, depending on the kind of jump? Or are they generally kept to a percentage increase?

—What is the policy on salary reviews? How often and when are they made? For example, is the first review six months or one year after the date of employment? Are subsequent reviews made on a calendar-year or anniversary-of-employment basis?

—What other forms of compensation are available (for example, bonuses, incentives, profit sharing)? How are these forms of compensation paid, when, and to whom? Are they paid in the event of voluntary or involuntary termination of employment?

When the timing seems right, be direct in making inquiries about compensation. Such questions are necessary and expected. Just because an organization doesn't open up and offer full information on its compensation policies is no reason not to ask for it; in fact, there's no justification for *not* asking. If interviewers fudge on their answers, watch out.

Here are some more areas you should get information about:

Insurance coverage. Don't just ask if the company has coverage; get details on the extent of it. Ask about life insurance, medical and surgical disability income, major medical insurance, accidental death and dismemberment coverage, dental expenses, prepaid legal expenses, automobile coverage.

Pension and retirement plans. This is a question women often do not ask (which only reinforces some males' convictions that women aren't really interested in a career). With the new vesting requirements established by law, there could be benefits for you even if you don't stay with the company until retirement.

Vacations, sick leave, personal leave, general holidays. Are they in line with what other companies and industries in the area offer? Can you carry over unused vacation until the following year? Don't forget to inquire about your ability to take a leave of absence if it becomes necessary.

Educational benefits. Some companies have a tuition-refund program whereby they will pay for all or part of your continued education. Clarify the extent to which such courses must be job-related.

Travel and entertainment expenses. Strictly speaking, this is not a compensation; you can't make money on most expense accounts. But if you are expected to travel or entertain for business purposes, you'll be interested in what restrictions the organization may put on you in terms of reimbursement.

Professional and club memberships. These can run into quite a bit of money. Thus, if a company is willing to provide them, such memberships constitute an attractive and competitive form of compensation.

If the interest is truly mutual, negotiating about compensation and discussing benefits and perquisites are not only legitimate but they reveal a great deal about your sense of your own worth. Bear in mind that if salary increases are going to be based on a percentage of your income, then the higher your base, the higher the increases.

How much of an increase over your present compensation should you ask for when you change jobs? There's no easy formula. Normally the switching premium for a young MBA is about 20 percent. If times are good and there's great demand for your skills, you might ask for as much as 30 percent. If you have to relocate, take that into consideration. It's not enough for your new employer to pay your transportation expenses. It may cost you more to live in the new area, so the new salary should be higher to allow for an increased cost of living—as well as to make up for the risks incurred in changing jobs and changing cities.

You may be told that others are being hired for the same kind of job at a lower salary, but don't let this inhibit you. Your salary demands should reflect what you believe you are worth. Most career-minded people agree on the importance of a discernible salary progression. If you can't get a job that will pay you what you think you're worth, you may be better off doing part-time, freelance, or unrelated work for a time until you find a suitable job. This isn't always true, of course. You may decide to take a job for less money than you prefer, if it seems promising enough. But if you agree to such a deal, make sure the benefits of the arrangement are real, and not a rationalization. For example, the job should by all indications lead to a much better position than you originally aimed for, or put you in close contact with powerful and influential people, or ultimately take you to even higher compensation levels than you originally were seeking.

JOB INTERVIEWING

Before actually going out on job interviews, there are a few preparatory steps you should take, in addition to developing a résumé and, if necessary, a portfolio, notebook, or folder of backup material. We have already suggested that you inform yourself about the company you will be seeing. You might also want to check up on employment agencies and search firms that handle jobs in your field, either by asking other people about them or by asking the agencies themselves for a brochure on the services they provide. In general, if several of your friends have used a firm or agency successfully, or you've heard good things about it, you don't have to inquire further.

It's very important that you look and feel well when you go on an important interview and that you be relaxed and not too rushed. So get a good night's sleep, give yourself enough time to get dressed at a leisurely pace in the morning, and allow ample time to get to your appointment. It's a good idea to allow a little extra time in case you have any difficulty locating the offices. As mentioned earlier, wear an outfit that is suitable for the job and that makes you feel attractive.

These are common-sense matters that practically everybody thinks about. What may be less obvious is that you should develop a sales presentation for yourself. The basic elements of this presentation will remain the same for all types of organizations, and they will cover the key information that companies want to know—your major strengths, the things you want and like to do, the reasons you want to leave your present employer and did leave previous ones, why you want to switch fields (if you do), why you seem to have an interest in the firm that is interviewing you, and your job or career goals. ("What job do you want to be doing five years from now?" is a standard question at interviews.)

But certain other aspects of your presentation should vary according to the position for which you are being interviewed and the organization. For example, if you're being seen by a marketing executive about a sales job, you'll need to emphasize the contact parts of your previous work, how much you like meeting new people and the challenge of visiting new towns (if travel is involved) and of figuring out the people and their interests so you can decide how to slant your sales pitch. If, on the other hand, you are applying for a desk job, you should probably indicate that you're good with details and enjoy working with figures or ideas. Similarly, if the job in which you're interested involves high-pressure activities, tight deadlines, and immediate results rather than low-pressure duties and long-term results, it's up to you to get the message across that this is what you like and do best.

The way you deliver the message is just as important as the message itself; in fact, for women it is often more important. Although you shouldn't come on like a super salesperson if you're angling for a non-sales job (especially if the man or woman talking to you is a soft-spoken, low-keyed person), you should be positive, pleasantly assertive, and ready to assume initiative if the conversation lags or veers off in the wrong direction.

A friend of ours told us about an interview she had for a job that required considerable contact with executives (and several skills she had not developed in previous jobs). At the beginning of the interview, the personnel manager jotted down on a piece of paper the most important requirement of the job and said that he'd show it to her at the end of the interview. When they had finished, he handed her the piece of paper, which said, "She will interview me." (She got the job.)

Generally, it's a good idea to work out your basic presentation, and then to try it out at a couple of relatively unimportant interviews, such as preliminary discussions with an employment agency or a firm that has an opening you know you don't want, before using it in an interview that is important to you. You can also rehearse your sales presentation or talk it through with a friend or business acquaintance. In some cases, it's not a bad idea to review your sales pitch and key sales points just before you go into an interview.

You should use whatever method works best for you and seems to produce the most effective results, since no one approach is appropriate for all job hunters. We offer here some suggestions that have worked well for many job applicants and that are recommended by a number of employment professionals. You can keep them in mind when you are developing your own interview techniques.

After the amenities are over and the initial questions are asked, allow the conversation to flow in whatever order the interviewer wishes. But should something you feel is important be overlooked, gently put the interviewer back on the track by asking if he or she would like the details that you want to make known. If the interviewer doesn't channel the conversation in the right direction, do it yourself, but very subtly.

Try to maintain a middle-of-the-road position in every way. Be enthusiastic and interested in the job and company but not excessively eager. Be relaxed and comfortable, but not casual or chummy. Be agreeable about extending the interview but not willing to let the interviewer take up your time by making you wait outside a long time, allowing innumerable interruptions, or prolonging the discussion way past the scheduled time. (There are many ways to handle these situations, such as "This seems to be a busy day for you. Would you like to arrange the appointment for another day?" Or, "I'd like to spend more time here but I have a two o'clock staff meeting.") In other words, be professional, friendly, courteous, and firm.

Avoid all forms of exaggeration about your own achievements and abilities, your status and that of your boss. Praise your boss and company, but not excessively—since the interviewer may begin to wonder or even ask you why you want to leave the company. Also, make sure your facts are correct. If the company is interested in you, they'll check up on your employment and education, and if you've provided false information, there'll be no job offer.

Emphasize your strong motivation and work orientation, your desire to work for an outstanding company, your need to learn and grow and gain new skills, your willingness to work hard and put in extra hours, to travel if necessary. And if your marital situation (being a wife and mother) seems to be on the interviewer's mind, and you are willing to discuss it (although legally you're not required to), say that it's not a problem and explain why.

Ask intelligent questions about the job, the department, the company, the industry, even the interviewer if it seems appropriate. Express interest in the facilities, view, furnishings (if they are outstanding). But don't ask too many questions or encourage a lot of chitchat or idle conversation.

Don't criticize your present or previous employers, even if they deserve it. If you feel it's absolutely necessary for you to explain that there is or was a conflict, do it in as impersonal a manner as possible, such as by commenting that the manager is rather authoritarian and several subordinates have resigned from this person's group because of this. Also, don't reveal any company secrets. If you're asked questions about your present or previous employers, give straightforward, knowledgeable answers, but no facts not known outside the company.

Don't discuss salary, benefits, or timing (when you would be available for employment), unless you are asked. If the interview ends with the next step up in the air, leave it there. Just say you enjoyed meeting your interviewer, and talking with him or her, then shake hands and leave.

By all means, shake hands with people when you meet and when you say goodbye—unless it's not possible, that is, if the person is barricaded behind a desk, is too far away, or shows signs of not wanting to shake hands. And be sure to give a firm handshake, not a limp, lifeless one.

Make an effort to remember the name of everyone you meet—including secretaries, since they can be most helpful when you place follow-up telephone calls and want to be sure you aren't disturbing the person you're calling.

Be polite and careful. Don't smoke unless the interviewer does and asks if you'd like to. When you're invited to lunch for a follow-up interview with several persons and you're asked if you want a drink, either decline or, if you have the menu, say you'd like to decide what you want to eat (so that someone else has to make the initial decision). If you're on the spot, say that a glass of wine might be pleasant.

Look your interviewer in the eye when you talk, but don't stare. If you can tell that direct eye contact makes the interviewer uncomfortable, it's probably a good idea to avoid it. Don't squirm or act restless, impatient, or bored, unless you want to ruin the interview.

Don't allow yourself to be pushed into accepting a job on the spot, without having time to think about it, or into discussing your background or providing personal information that is none of the company's business.

According to Title VII of the Civil Rights Act of 1964, as amended by the Equal Employment Opportunity Act of 1972, companies are not supposed to ask you about your marital status, how many children you have, how old they are, whether you are pregnant, or even how you feel about pregnancy and children. They also shouldn't ask how long you've lived at your current address, or whether you have a driver's license or own a car. Nor should they ask your race, height, weight, hair color, or eye color. If they do ask these questions (and they may), they run the risk of being accused of discrimination.

Title VII also prohibits companies from asking these questions: Where were you born? Are you a naturalized citizen of the United States? Do you speak a foreign language? If so, where did you learn it? What are the names of your brothers, sisters, parents, or other relatives? What lodges, clubs, and societies do you belong to? What holidays do you observe? What church do you belong to? Have you ever been arrested? And, of course, questions about your age and requests for proof of age or a photograph are prohibited.

In developing an effective job-hunting strategy, the importance of doing your homework—knowing your strengths, the direction your abilities and interests should take you, and the realities of the business world—cannot be too strongly emphasized. If you project self-confidence and clarity of thinking in your résumé and your interviews, this will go a long way toward convincing interviewers that you're worth considering—and on your own terms.

REFERENCE

1. Larry E. Suter and Herman P. Miller, ''Income Difference Between Men and Career Women,'' *American Journal of Sociology,* January 1973, pp. 967–968.

7

GETTING ON THE FAST TRACK

ONCE inside an organization, the would-be achiever can make one or more mistakes. She can:

—depend too heavily on the organizational management to provide upward paths for her, perhaps through their affirmative action plan.

—develop a close relationship with her boss and become too much of an extension of him or her.

—become too comfortable and/or expert in one job and rationalize her failure to push on.

—engage in career planning sporadically, perhaps only when she is restless and dissatisfied.

—become so engrossed in job responsibilities that she fails to see opportunities opening up.

—neglect to broadcast her ambitions and abilities to the right ears.

These are just a few of the many possible pitfalls. The ambitious woman must recognize the need to plan on a continuing basis, to assess her capacities periodically, to set timetables. She needs to know how and when to move—and what kind of a move to make. And she does not rest between moves. She works to enlarge her responsibilities, to learn as much as she can, to get as close to the centers of power and influence as possible.

HALF-TRUTHS ABOUT GETTING AHEAD

Mary Wells Lawrence, who heads the advertising agency Wells Rich Greene Inc., is considered good copy, because she is an attractive blonde in her forties, bright, chic, and, of course, very successful.

In much that is written about her, however, there is the sly implication that her fast rise was really due to . . . well, after all, you're bound to get ahead if you marry your biggest client. Because that is what she did; she married Harding L. Lawrence, chief executive of Braniff International. That airline was the account with which Mrs. Lawrence achieved fame when she was with another agency. When she left to start her own shop, Braniff followed. So did Mr. Lawrence.

It's true that there are times when romance may help. But in Mrs. Lawrence's case, there were large amounts of ambition, intelligence, shrewdness, timing, organizational ability, and other talents to help her reach the point where she is now the highest paid advertising executive in the United States.

Unfortunately, the marry-the-big-client (or boss) theory is only one of several half-truths about what it takes to get ahead in organizational life. Basing one's advancement strategy on any one of them is pretty chancy; and, in view of today's business climate, it is surprising that they are still in existence. But exist they do, each with its loyal coterie.

Three of these myths might be considered part of the "good girl" syndrome. Basically, the theme of each is "Just sit tight—and, sooner or later, you'll get your reward." Is it true? Let's take a closer look at the theories.

The Cinderella theory. An advocate of this theory, an administrative assistant, is going to stand in for her boss in making a presentation to the executive committee. Looking ahead to the big day, she imagines the executives saying, ''Who is she? What talent! We must promote her to an important position.''

There are several problems with this viewpoint. First, the executives on the committee expect a good presentation, no matter who makes it. Furthermore, most of the credit for the presentation will go to the assistant's boss. And, finally, it takes more than one appearance to make a ''star.'' If this administrative assistant wants to move up in the organizational hierarchy, she will need assistance and encouragement from her boss—and much more visibility within the company.

The cream theory. From time to time, the belief is expressed that the best (most talented, most intelligent, most . . .) will automatically rise to the top.

However, a close look at business organizations will show that many executives have come from upper middle class homes, have graduated from certain universities, and have traveled well-worn paths through finance or marketing. Whatever the criteria most frequently applied, they did not necessarily include superiority in intelligence, ability, or managerial skills.

And it is risky to assume that people who occupy the upward tracks are going to move aside willingly. Studies show that persons with the most management potential may indeed move a great deal, but not necessarily in a straight line. There is much lateral motion, and considerable amounts of thinking and planning usually go into whatever direction is next contemplated.

The Puritan ethic. Work hard, don't make waves, walk the straight and narrow—and you are bound to be rewarded. As a way of life it sounds very noble, but the realities of the business world reveal its flaws.

In almost every organization, there are any number of people who have worked hard and become known for their reliability. Alas, few of them rise very far in the hierarchy, because that term ''reliable'' tags them as good and desirable *subordinates*. A manager who is lucky enough to have such good employees often prefers to have them stay right where they are.

The three theories of advancement just detailed involve their proponents in essentially passive roles—they sit back and wait for lightning to strike. Here are two theories that stress more active participation—of one kind or another:

The jungle theory. This, of course, is the survival of the fittest, the strongest, the most competitive, the most political. Leadership of the pack goes to the person who outwits his competitors, by-passes slower colleagues, responds quickly to major changes.

There's no question that people who want to get ahead should sense the organizational climate, know what kinds of behavior and attributes are most favored by those in power. However, in most instances, the person who tramples on others while racing to be leader will get only so far before co-workers, peers and superiors, will find ways of keeping this unscrupulous individual from getting too close to his or her goal. Their instincts for self-protection—the feeling that the hard-driver is a threat to them and the positions they hold—spur them to action.

The starlet theory. According to this theory, a woman's sexual appeal (and use of it) will help her to progress in her career.

Undoubtedly some women have gotten to the top this way. But not enough is known about them to form conclusions about whether their careers were really aided by cashing in on good looks and a good figure, flirting, playing the poor-little-me role, or having an affair. Keep this in mind: establishing a career is uncertain and complicated at best, and it becomes even more so when sex enters the picture.

These theories, and others like them, are not reliable guides for advancement. Every now and then, of course, there are exceptions that almost make them ring true. An especially promising person does become an overnight success; or a ruthless executive does slice and stomp his way to the top. But they are still only exceptions. They don't occur often enough to lend any credence to the theories.

But if Cinderella isn't going to make it and Ruthless Rita is going to be cut down in the home stretch, who is going to get to the top? The answers are as varied as the individuals themselves, but, generally speaking, most successful people have a number of things in common:

1. They don't sit on the sidelines and wait for things to happen. Neither do they knock down fences or badger people unnecessarily. But they do make constructive efforts to be visible—willingly taking on new and challenging assignments, expanding contacts with people, volunteering for committees, and so on. They are always with—and part of—the action.

2. They have a very clear idea of their worth. This doesn't mean that they think they're indispensable or smarter and more knowledgeable than others. They realize that they have much to learn, but they are quietly confident of their ability to take on whatever comes along.

3. They have definite goals and know where they want to go. There is little shilly-shallying or confusion for these people. They've surveyed the scene, assessed the alternatives, and decided on a course of action.

4. They are always looking for ways to improve, to help them achieve their goals. What will it take—further studies, new skills, a different environment, more time on certain projects? They get the answer—and act on it.

For most of them, the road up is long, arduous, well-conceived, and well-executed—if not always exciting or sensational. And few of the successful ones ever stop working at it, even when they've reached the top.

EXAMINING THE ORGANIZATION CHART

The entire range of opportunities in any organization is never spelled out in a chart. However, once you have a fix on your own needs and goals, the next step is to determine what may be available in your organization. You cannot do that, of course, unless you know the operation of which you are a part.

As you look at the organization chart, you may be tempted to select—or reject—the areas that you feel offer the least opportunity. Resist that temptation, however, and try to evaluate the channels of advancement as if you didn't know the organization, as if you were coming to the chart "cold." In doing this, you may find that for one reason or another (for example, a particular manager's expressed antifeminist bias) you have neglected to consider a route or position for which you are qualified. The question to ask about every channel, therefore, is "Why not?" You may discover that more paths are open to you than you had thought possible.

You may also want to consult other people about job possibilities. They may be able to help you see some opportunities that you missed.

Does your company offer a tuition refund program that you can use to further your education or training? Have you expressed any interest in it? In many companies, educational and training opportunities are available, but few employees know about them or take advantage of them. Furthermore, some executives never think of suggesting to a woman that she take a course or seminar. She has to show evidence of her drive by specifically asking to be sent to the course.

Do you read the periodicals that are circulated within the company? You can learn a lot about your field from them. Perhaps you can get your name added to the routing lists. If not, you can certainly read those that find their way to your boss's desk.

If you have a company library, you can browse through it to discover what might interest or aid you. Your local public library can also provide you with useful material. For guidance, consult the librarians and also people who work in the specific areas in which you are interested.

The questions we've presented here are designed to help you focus on some of the opportunities available in your organization. After you have thought about them, let other people in on your thinking. Essential to advancement in most organizations is visibility—that is, getting the attention of those who can open the doors for you and letting them know, indirectly or directly, that you're eager to learn and progress.

DRAWING ATTENTION TO YOURSELF

There is a quaint notion that the only truly effective way to achieve visibility is to demonstrate talent by doing an outstanding job. Proving you are exceptionally competent is one way to get the attention of people who can be influential in your career progress. However, competence often needs—is certainly enhanced by— some good public relations. If you are fortunate, you can get some of your publicizing done by others. For example, if you are a val- ued subordinate, and if your superiors realize that applause for you is applause for them, most of them will let people up the line know about you.

Your peers—some of them—will talk you up (just as your subor- dinates will), but usually only if they like you *and* respect you *and* trust you *and* do not regard you as a threat. The problem with pub- licity from this source is that you cannot control it or depend on it. And it may not get far enough. But when it does reach influential ears, it can have an impact, especially if it comes from people who do not—ostensibly, at least—have a vested interest in your prog- ress.

You can achieve a good deal of helpful publicity for yourself. If your conditioning and upbringing have discouraged you from call- ing attention to yourself, you have your work cut out for you. Your first step is to decide just whom you want to impress favorably. Shotgun blasts are sometimes effective—and, of course, the more widely known your name the better it is for you; someone you are not now acquainted with may hear about you and be quite influen- tial in your career at a future date. Generally, however, you'll want to take every opportunity to tailor information about yourself to the needs, interests, and responsibilities of those within the organiza- tion who could be involved in making decisions about your future: those who are power centers.

FINDING THE POWER CENTERS

In mapping out the fast track, it is usually helpful to know where the power centers are in the organization. Who are the managers with the most influence and prestige? Who are the people involved in the important decision-making?

There are good reasons to study the power people. For one thing, the closer you get to them the better the chances that they will be instrumental in furthering your career. Also, they often manifest the organization's value system—the kinds of achievements, specializations, and behavior patterns that most frequently get rewarded within the organization. In addition, it is possible that the people who report to them have the best opportunities for moving ahead.

The power people are not always the ones with the big titles, who move in the spotlight, whose names are well known. Here are some indicators for learning just who has the power. Who:

—has made significant upward progress in the company?
—is always being quoted?
—chairs the important meetings, writes the significant memos, makes the really informative major announcements?
—is frequently consulted by other managers and specialists?
—always seems to have the latest information about what is going on and who is doing what?
—is frequently seen conferring or communicating with, or in the company of, the top brass?
—answers questions from insiders and outsiders without having to get help from others?
—has a lot of responsibility and looks comfortable with it?

PUTTING YOUR NAME BEFORE THE RIGHT PEOPLE

It is important that you get your name before the proper people and keep it there. Some of the tips we offer are so simple and obvious that they are often overlooked as promotion aids. Others are considerably more involved and take planning. You want to avoid coming across as too eager and transparent in your publicizing. Some experienced managers consider an intensive public relations campaign as a warning that there is less there than meets the eye— the talents of some people are largely confined to the selling of themselves.

Using names. There is nothing more flattering than to be called by name. Women very often don't call men they don't know well by their names. But greeting people by name and showing them that you know who they are is a good way to get attention. Men have become accustomed to making the first moves to know women; as a woman, you'll usually find it advantageous to make that first move. And when you meet men inside or outside the organization, shake hands, since men are used to this kind of contact during the introduction process. You'll find that most men appreciate your efforts to take the initiative in communicating with them the same way another man would.

Offering ideas and suggestions. Test your ideas first on others whose judgment you trust. You may hear that what counts is getting people to listen to your ideas, not the feasibility of those ideas. (The rationale is that the ideas will probably be rejected anyway, but at least you'll have had somebody's attention.) But there are managers who resent being imposed on with ideas that can't be implemented. Furthermore, ideas that aren't well thought out or whose consequences are not sufficiently anticipated by their originator may suggest that she is not conversant with the needs and functions of the organization. So before you submit an idea or suggestion up the line, be sure it's sound and salable. You should be able to tell the recipients why the idea should be considered, how they and/or the organization could benefit from it, what resources it would involve, such as time, money, and personnel, and what negative factors or disadvantages are inherent in the idea and how those can be alleviated or offset.

Usually the best way to present an idea or suggestion is through your immediate superior. Even if your boss can't or won't help you, he or she can hurt your chances of getting your idea before the right people. So, if you bypass your boss, make sure you have permission to do so, or a good reason—for example, he or she is to be away for an extended time.

Writing memos. The strategy of sending memos and copies of memos can be overdone. That's especially true of FYI (for your information) memos. They usually just get filed or discarded. If you believe a memo you have written to someone in your department would be of interest to a manager or other influential person, send him a copy of it, especially if the memo refers to the recipient or his function, or relates to an interesting or unusual project that might affect his work. Be sure to attach a brief note explaining why you thought of the person. If someone who reports to you sends you a memo with a suggestion, forward it up the line with your comments. That way you become represented as heading up a department that has innovative people in it—or at least people who are involved and concerned.

Recommending articles, books, and other reading material. Generally reading matter gets distributed from above. But it needn't be one way. If you read something —usually, though not necessarily, work-related—that can provide an idea or stimulation for someone else, even a superior, send the person a copy or a note referring to it, and explain why you're recommending it. However, unless you're fairly well acquainted with the person, use this technique judiciously. Otherwise you may be viewed as too pushy; or, if the superior in question is a man, he may think you're personally interested in him.

Committees and projects. Volunteer or at least be available for service on task forces, committees, and planning groups that may not directly contribute to your primary work responsibilities. For example, if there is to be an annual conference of key managers, you might offer to help. Such work can be bothersome, but it can also put you before the right people. An unusual event, a particularly entertaining meeting, hospitable facilities, an enjoyable break in the routine are remembered for years. And so is the person responsible for them. So, any kind of group activity that will be in the spotlight or cross organizational boundaries is worth considering. The tendency of most people to shy away from activities that are not directly related to their usual functions is a break for the person who wants to use such opportunities for a bit of personal public relations.

Running meetings. If you are in charge of a meeting, consider inviting an influential superior to sit in, or persuade the person who is in charge to let you do so. Obviously this technique will only be effective if the person will be interested in the session and not feel his or her time has been wasted. Also, you'll want to make sure that the person leaves with a dominant impression of your competence and group skills.

Using bulletin boards and internal publications. Complimentary letters and memos about your activities, productivity statistics, charts that show comparative performance—all have a legitimate place on the bulletin board in your department or in some other visible location. If you have something to report about yourself for an internal publication—a seminar you've attended, a field trip you were on, a talk you've given, an article you've written—mention it to the editor so it can be written up.

Participating in community activities. An advantage of working in a small town or city is that you can more easily participate in important community activities and report those activities in the local newspaper. Take every opportunity to have your name and picture printed in local publications that will be seen by influentials. When you read something about an influential member of your organization, clip out the article and send it to him or her with your comments or congratulations.

Promoting other women. We have heard women in responsible positions say, "I don't give a damn about the other women, just myself"; or "I've been encouraged not to have too much contact with other women in the organization." But there are dangers in isolation. Other women can be resources to you. If you acknowledge them, assist them, get recognition for them, you may run the risk of aiding a potential competitor, but it's also possible that you'll win yourself an ally—and you can never discount the chance that one of those women might move fast and far enough to open doors for you later.

If it becomes known that you are a source of knowledge about the women in the organization who might be candidates for bigger jobs, you then become more valuable. You will be consulted, your evaluations solicited.

Many women will find that it is to their advantage to promote the cause of other able women. More women in responsible positions in an organization means an easier time for all women, not a more difficult one—except, of course, in the competition for very top jobs, a level on which both men and women find the struggle difficult.

However, it is important to bear in mind that championing the cause of other women must always be done from the perspective of supporting *all* able people, whether women or men. If you are partial toward women, over the long pull it will prove self-defeating. You can lose valuable potential friends and allies—and possibly do a disservice to the organization.

Your attempts at increasing your visibility to influential superiors are enhanced every time you can initiate an idea, suggestion, or proposal up the line or on a broader basis than your boss represents. The further your ideas go, however, the less control you can exercise over them. Since you won't want to relinquish all ownership or control, you should find ways to get yourself included in the deliberations and the decision-making process.

GETTING ACTION UP THE LINE

After you've made a proposal, there may be extensive delays before any action is taken, since the different schedules of the people who will discuss it may not allow them to meet for quite some time. And, understandably, their order of priorities is probably not the same as yours.

As time passes, you may begin to wonder what, if anything, is happening to your request or proposal. In that case, the first thing to do is to ask your boss what he or she knows about the situation. Has consideration bogged down—and why? If it has, what can you do to get the wheels turning again?

What you're after, of course, is a reason to reopen the deliberations. Chances are you didn't use all of your ammunition in your original request. Undoubtedly, there was at least one "selling point" you left out. Or perhaps there has been an additional development that might affect your proposal. Anything in the areas of cost, application, newly discovered benefits that could justify saying, "Here's something else that should be considered," can be used as a door opener.

Once you have a good reason to send waves up the line, there are a variety of steps you can take to get yourself as close to the decision making as possible.

You might say to your boss: "Let's set up a meeting so we can explain this new benefit." Your aim, of course, is to make sure you'll do the talking about your proposal rather than someone else.

There's always something "lost in the translation" when another person has to speak for you. It's altogether possible, too, that you'll find that someone else (your boss, perhaps) is relieved to have you do the explaining.

A slightly less direct approach is to suggest a meeting and then say: "Let me tag along to the meeting, just in case." You may find this more diplomatic, and at least you'll be there to see that everything you want said will be said. Before the meeting takes place, discuss with your boss how you can be an effective resource to him. That way you may be able to play a more active role in the deliberations.

Writing a memo to stir up the decision-making machinery is usually not as effective as participating in a meeting with higher managers. A memo can be set aside or buried—it doesn't have any great urgency about it. But it does give you a chance to get your ideas across in your own words. Address the memo to your boss so he or she can pass it along; conclude with an offer to discuss the matter personally with anyone who wishes to do so.

Another possibility is to suggest to your boss that the two of you talk directly with *his* boss. In this effort to get a decision out of those to whom your boss reports, you have to proceed with tact. However, your boss may have reason to welcome this direct approach. For example, your boss may be too busy to do your proposal justice—and he or she would be happy if you took matters into your own hands. In any event, if your boss knows that your words and actions will reflect favorably on him, you may get the go-ahead to meet and talk with the superior on your own.

GETTING YOUR AMBITIONS ACROSS

Suppose you hear of a job opening in your organization—and you think you'd be right for it. But you realize that ability is not enough. You also have to convince your boss and others that you should be promoted or transferred into the job. This requires a thorough analysis along the following lines:

Find out as much about the position as possible. What does the job entail in the way of credentials and duties? Who will select the person to fill it? What criteria will be used in making that selection?

List the experience and skills you have that would qualify you for consideration. For example, if you were applying for a job training editorial assistants, your experience as a successful editor would be an important consideration, but the fact that you taught school for two years before becoming an editor might be a greater asset. Play devil's advocate by forcing yourself to demonstrate proof of accomplishment and evidence that your skills are all they should be.

Develop a sales presentation. This is the step that many women overlook. However, a series of thoughtful, well-presented arguments that show why you feel you are qualified for the job can make a tremendous impression on the people who are making the decision.

In developing your presentation, think about the following questions: Why do you want the job? How can you best demonstrate your qualifications? What would getting the job mean—for you and the organization? The presentation needn't be terribly long, and it can be made verbally or in writing. Just be sure you know what you want to get across—and why.

Find out what your boss and others think of your chances. Listen carefully, because you will probably get some indications of the factors that will be most important. You may also learn about certain qualifications you haven't thought of. If so, you can inquire about those additional qualifications then and there—or in a later discussion.

Ask what steps still have to be taken before the decision is made. Perhaps additional applicants have to be interviewed. Or another manager may have to be consulted. Or a "test" assignment may have to be completed. Find out what still has to be done, what "campaigning" you can do in the meantime, and what further evidence of your interest and ability you can manifest.

Follow up during the decision-making period. "Camping out on the doorstep" is not recommended. However, a memo, a telephone call, an expressed willingness to supply more information—all these can be effective in focusing the decision-maker's attention on your candidacy. They also show your genuine interest in the job.

One specific suggestion concerning this follow-up: when you call or write, try to avoid merely asking where you stand. Open the conversation with an inquiry about another subject or an item of information you haven't yet disclosed. This gives your call a purpose, an immediacy, a reason for the person making the decision to think anew about your qualifications.

In working for a promotion or a change of job, keep your name and your assets before the people who will make the choice. It would be nice if they found you such a talented, experienced applicant that there was no way they could overlook you. However, you can't depend on that. Remember that others may be doing all they can to help the decision-makers forget about you.

RECEIVING A PROMOTION

Understandably, most upwardly mobile persons welcome an opportunity to move up the line. Therefore, they emphasize the pluses and play down the minuses of the move, in the hope that, fully prepared or not, they will be able to handle the new job. Some succeed, of course, but others do not. They are not ready—or, in some cases, they are not really willing—to take on greater challenges and responsibilities.

When you are offered a promotion, therefore, you might do well to consider the following questions before you make your decision:

Have you assessed how your own needs match the organizational needs reflected in the job? An assistant marketing manager was offered the job of trainer in another division of her corporation. Her responsibility, a substantial one, would be to help build a national sales staff of women to demonstrate products at retail outlets and trade shows. Both the salary and the prestige appealed to her, but the fact that she would have to spend more time in the field with the salespeople did not. In addition, this manager had a growing interest in public relations and advertising. Her needs would probably be frustrated in the sales position.

Most people need to redefine their needs and goals periodically. No fast-track person can afford to assume that just because she has done well in a particular line of work she will also do well in a more responsible position in that line. Nor can she automatically assume that the type of work she has enjoyed doing thus far will continue to satisfy her indefinitely.

How well prepared are you to take on the new responsibilities? Suppose, for example, you have always worked in engineering and a great new marketing position opens up. It involves a product you know intimately, and you are attracted by the opportunity. However, the new job requires an extensive knowledge of finance and statistics, as well as some background in the psychology of buyer motivation. That's a lot of knowledge to acquire in a short time while you are trying to run the operation. If you are not prepared now, how much time will you have to gain the knowledge you will need? Is that time period realistic?

Is the job performable? It is entirely possible that the job has grown too big for one individual to handle it. Or the responsibility it entails may drastically exceed the authority you will have.

Suppose, for example, that a new department has been created. For the time being, the permanent staff will be small in order to keep costs down. The manager of this department will have to negotiate for more people on a shared basis. She will not have any real authority over these people, nor will she be able to remonstrate if they fail to contribute in proportion to her needs. Yet she will be expected to maintain a certain output regardless of her lack of authority. This is a situation that could tax the most experienced manager.

Another difficulty in handling a higher position is the variety in the quality of support you can expect from bosses, colleagues, and employees. It isn't only a matter of transferring or developing loyalty. Other people may simply be too busy—due to fast-changing events or understaffing—to give you much help during your period of transition. Consequently, you may find the new job and your aloneness in it overwhelming.

Are you emotionally ready for the promotion? This may be a

very difficult question to answer because it requires a great deal of honesty on your part. You may be intellectually qualified and still be emotionally unable to handle the job.

We're not talking about neuroses, but rather the kind of emotional problems that many people experience from time to time. Domestic troubles or ill health can cut down on one's ability to cope emotionally. So can boredom, or confusion in career planning. Taking a new job simply to escape from the old one may result in even greater boredom or confusion.

One thing is pretty certain: if an employee is having problems dealing with her present responsibilities, changing those responsibilities or taking on increased burdens will not necessarily resolve her difficulties.

Is the increase in salary big enough to free you from any additional financial burdens that the new job entails? Suppose, for example, you now work in Boston and you're offered a position in Chicago. Will the increased salary make the move worthwhile—or will you sink deeper into a financial quagmire?

It isn't only the moving expenses and the new house or apartment that must be considered. There may be other expenses as well. For example, in your new position will you be expected to lunch more frequently at expensive restaurants? Will you be required to entertain more lavishly or join a club? If so, how will these bills be handled? Will your expense account cover them? And what about your family: Will some members have to make the move with you? It's better to find out now than to trust that things will work out later.

When you are offered a promotion, consider all the angles carefully. Then, if you decide to say yes, try to make the kind of deal that will give you enough money, time, and space to make the move worthwhile.

MISSING A PROMOTION

Losing out on a desired promotion is more than a simple disappointment. The loss of a higher salary, a more impressive title, and enlarged authority are only the most obvious deprivations. You also have been deprived of such important intangibles as the knowledge that people up the line hold you in esteem, that they recognize your true value—as you see it. You are denied the reassuring signal that you can and will get ahead in your career. Instead of the reward you craved, you've been given a very solid blow to your self-esteem.

But in the loss of a much-desired promotion, the choice is not between keeping a stiff upper lip and slitting your throat. Instead, this is a time for a realistic assessment of what went wrong, so that you can plan present and future conduct that will minimize your chances of having to face a similar disappointment later on.

You shouldn't pretend that your emotions aren't involved. They are. But there's a difference between keeping emotions under control and totally ignoring their existence. On the other hand, you should keep your disappointment in perspective. It's not the end of the world. Life offers many more satisfactions than one particular job can possibly provide, even if you really wanted the promotion.

Turn aside, politely, the people who want to commiserate with you. Recognize that this form of sympathy is almost always self-serving. Now is the time to think about the image you project. No matter how battered you may feel, show the world a calm, balanced self-confidence.

When the immediate effects of the blow to your ego have passed, make an objective evaluation of why you weren't chosen for the position and someone else was. If at the end of this evaluation, you honestly feel you have the talents for the job you didn't get, why weren't they recognized? Did the person who got the promotion get it through politics, apple-polishing, or back-stabbing? If so, how can you guard against a similar maneuver by someone else in the future? Was discrimination—based on race, religion, or sex—a major factor? If so, do you have the will and personal strength to seek legal redress, knowing what the company's reaction will be?

On the other hand, if you come to realize that you really were not the best person for that particular job, what skills do you have that will win you future promotion?

After enough time has elapsed for you to be sure you can keep the conversation totally objective, let your boss know of your disappointment. In this way, you have not only made your "availability" for a higher position clear; you also have a chance to get pointers on what you must do to qualify for future promotion.

GAINING RECOGNITION AFTER A PROMOTION

Gaining recognition in a new job can be very difficult, particularly when no problems have been anticipated. People tend to regard their promotions as a kind of edict to the world. Let the word go out (in a discreetly flattering memo) that Jones has just been appointed head of the department, and it should be perfectly clear, so Jones feels, just where and how she now fits into the organization. People will recognize her new authority, appreciate her new responsibilities, automatically change their image of her from assistant to head.

The fact is, of course, that a promotion doesn't bring about any overnight changes—in the person just promoted, or in the people who work with her. New title notwithstanding, Jones is still the same person, with the same image. And that is exactly the way people will continue to see her, with little or no change in their relationships with her, until—and unless—she makes the adjustments necessary for assuming her new role.

For each step you take up the organizational ladder, you should develop a definite strategy as to how you will act in the new position—in order to get the kind of reaction you want from others. In developing that strategy, consider the following:

Your image of yourself. Although you are pleased with your new title, new salary, and new authority, are you still thinking and acting in the same way you did before—typing your own letters even though there is someone else available to do them; automatically assuming that you will take the notes in a meeting with your male colleagues; volunteering to make the luncheon arrangements for the next conference? These are easy traps to fall into, particularly during those first days and weeks when you still haven't definitely settled into the new job.

Yet these first impressions could be lasting ones, with people finding it difficult to see you in anything but your old role. If you want to have the recognition that goes with your new job, you have to act as though you belong in it—right from the start.

Your view of the new job. In many companies, job descriptions are vague at best; they seem to vary from individual to individual, from department to department. If you don't have a clear definition of your new responsibilities, you may run into serious problems, not only about what tasks you should or should not be doing, but also over conflicts in authority and jurisdiction.

It may require some digging, even some pestering, to get all the information you need. But once you have it, you will be in a better position to tackle the job in a way that will help to build the image you want to achieve.

Your expertness. "What can you do for me?" is the name of a vital and omnipresent organizational game. The more assistance you render colleagues, the more willing they will be to accept you in your new role.

At the start of a new job, some people hesitate to admit to all the skills and abilities they possess. They are afraid that others will consider them braggarts or know-it-alls. Yet why not provide expert assistance whenever you can? It's one way of showing your co-workers that you have the qualifications for the job.

Your relationship with former associates. Women seem to have a special problem in this area. In the company cafeteria, for example, they will sit down with other women—even if these women are on a lower job level—rather than join the men who are now their peers. Associations and friendships on the old level are comforting; they don't have to be given up. But it is only when you start making associations on the new level that people will begin to feel you belong there.

Your reaction—if you are bypassed or ignored. Unfortunately, many women find that although their new responsibilities have been detailed and their new authority clearly defined, they are being bypassed or ignored on matters that are of concern to them. An employee on a lower level goes around them to someone higher up. A top executive goes to one of their colleagues for information instead of coming to them.

If you find yourself in this position, you should speak out and make your position clear. Usually you don't have to do it angrily. A straightforward explanation of the facts of the situation will do. This should be done as soon as the problem occurs, because the longer you wait to assert yourself, the more difficult it will be to do so.

True recognition from people both up and down the line seldom comes with a promotion. It takes time—and effort on your part. But the better and more effective your strategy for projecting the right image in your new job, the sooner that recognition will come—and the sooner you can start thinking about your next move.

8

BUILDING
SKILLS

In many organizations a woman who wants to get ahead must show more drive and skill than a man who wants to move up. We offer in this chapter a basic checklist of personal skills needed in almost any kind of position and career. Mastery of these skills will not automatically propel a woman upward through an organization. But it will be extremely difficult for her to get ahead without them.

MANAGING YOUR TIME

The management of time is a good place to start. Peter Drucker, the well-known consultant, has said that most people really don't know how they invest their time—although they very often believe they do know. Chances are that if you kept a log for a week, accurately listing what you did with each quarter-hour, you would be startled to find how much more time you spent on certain tasks than you would have estimated in the beginning, and how much less time on others. It never fails to surprise people that how they think they spend time is at considerable variance with how they actually do spend it.

At the heart of any successful effort to manage time is the ability to set priorities. The problem, however, is *whose* priorities? For example, the boss comes to her assistant and says, "In the staff meeting today we discussed the possibility of consolidating the field sales operation of our division with the Thermocel group. What I'd like you to do is to give me your estimate of what our internal personnel needs would be if we went that route."

The assistant senses the boss's enthusiasm over the prospect, and puts aside her other duties to work on this special assignment. But the customers' correspondence lies there, suppliers' inquiries go unanswered, the specifications from engineering don't get examined and approved.

Another pitfall in controlling time is assigning equal value to each task. It is almost impossible to break into the schedule of a person who does this. The regimen is set, and any new task or special project waits its turn.

A third problem people often create for themselves derives from the belief that they must do everything that comes their way. The boss brings you a special project; a colleague prevails on you to help her out in a job "because everyone knows how good you are at it"; a subordinate comes to you for help and you wind up doing the job yourself; the people from the local drive for the leukemia fund implore you to take over as chairperson, and you accept.

You can easily get swept along—unless you develop realistic criteria to help you determine which tasks you will do yourself, which you will ask others to do, and which you will refuse to do altogether. In setting up these criteria, consider the following:

Your own goals. There are, of course, certain objectives you want to accomplish through your performance on the job—advancement, learning and expertness, esteem, professional recognition, money. Each task that you have to perform—or believe you have to perform—should be viewed in this perspective. Could the successful, high-quality performance of it have a positive influence on the attainment of your goals, a negative or blocking influence, or no applicable effect one way or the other?

The goals of the organization. First, is everything that you do called for in your job description? Second, do your day-to-day duties contribute materially to the objectives that you and your boss have spelled out and agreed upon? Many tasks may have little or nothing to do with your goals. It is a familiar tendency of people rising in organizations to take certain functions with them as they go—even though they performed those functions at lower levels. It may be time to ask others to maintain those marketing or personnel reports. Or perhaps certain supplies could be requisitioned by a subordinate.

Visibility. Some tasks provide a higher profile than others, which is an especially important consideration for the aspiring woman. Also, a task that will not bring immediate benefits has to be evaluated in terms of the long-range advantage it might offer.

Credit. Just as a politician collects IOUs when campaigning for a colleague or supporting another's legislation, you can accumulate a certain amount of credit for whatever assistance you give another, even though there is no immediate benefit accruing to you from the time you have invested.

Your various job duties should be measured against these considerations. Make a list of everything you do, and a log of how much time you spend doing it. Then take the following steps:

1. What tasks seem to be relatively unimportant? It might be time to consult with your boss and ask for their elimination or diminution.

2. What are you doing that a subordinate could do? A task that seems trivial or uninteresting to you could very well be a welcome change for someone who reports to you.

3. When assignments come your way, find out when they have to be completed. Don't take it for granted that everything has to be done immediately. You may have more time than you think.

4. When work comes your way that seems unpleasant or terribly complicated and for which you have a long deadline, let it simmer a while. Let your intuition work on it. You may come up with a method that would simplify it for you. Procrastination also gives you time to talk about the problem and to elicit suggestions from others.

5. Learn to say no. If the job really doesn't suit you and if you don't have to do it, develop ways to turn it down. This is especially true of social and outside activities—lunch dates, school and community events, charity drives.

6. Know the resources available to you. Know where you can go for help when you need it—who has what skill; who has slack time at the moment; what staff specialists are available to help.

7. Carve out large blocks of time when you need to. Perhaps you can alert your secretary and/or assistants to intercept all phone calls or visitors for a day. Take work home. Come in earlier in the morning. You will be surprised at how much productivity you can add to your day by coming in just a half-hour earlier. And if that extra half-hour (or hour) occurs before the switchboard is open, better yet. Part of that time should be spent organizing the work to be done that day.

8. Go with your biorhythm. There are times you may not feel intellectually, emotionally, or physically up to doing an important piece of work or starting a project. It's a good idea not to if you can afford to postpone it. If you push yourself to do it right then, it might take you much longer than if you did it when you were really up to it. You may only need to postpone it until the next morning or the day after that. The point is that you have ample evidence of your energy peaks, when you are more receptive to challenge, when you tend to feel more optimistic. That's the time to start a difficult task.

9. Break a difficult task into smaller units. If you are preparing a lengthy and involved report, break it into sections. The completion of each section will give you a sense of accomplishment, which in turn will contribute to a feeling of confidence that you will get through the following sections. Reward yourself. Take a break to do something you enjoy. Perhaps you'd like to take a short walk, talk to someone casually, read a magazine, do some work you enjoy doing.

10. You probably spend more time than you should in your reading. Learn to skim. Most people read far more than they have to. What can you file for future reference, when the content may be more relevant? What would happen if you did not read this? Very

often, not much at all. Save your lighter and more enjoyable reading for the end of the day, for the morning, for when you are tired, or for when you can't start a new project.

SOLVING PROBLEMS

Although there are numerous courses, books, and patented techniques available today to help the organization person with problem-solving, it is still worth discussing here. The difficulty with problem-solving as a highly valued skill is that it often engenders a frame of mind that is satisfied with keeping the status quo. Essentially, solving a problem is a corrective measure—you have gotten off course and you need to get back on. Restoring the status quo is quite sufficient for many people. In fact you can find some groups of people who are happy to have the same rather comfortable problems to deal with time after time. They become hobbies or forms of escape from unfamiliar, harsher realities.

Furthermore, problems have negative connotations. Say to someone, "You seem to have a problem," and you may get an unfriendly, unappreciative response. And many people duck problems because they feel that causes must be found and blame assigned. Some people confuse solving a problem with pointing out the culprit who was responsible for the error.

A more fruitful approach is to think in terms of goals rather than problems, alternatives rather than causes. A goal is something one reaches out for; it stimulates progressive, rather than corrective, thinking. Similarly, thinking in terms of what conditions you would prefer to see exist may lead to far greater improvement than that gained when the cause of a deviation is removed.

Problems and their causes do need to be identified, defined, and analyzed. But in any problem-solving situation, progress is made and leadership manifested when a person focuses on the following questions:

—What alternative to the present situation would I prefer to see? (You may be talking about different conditions, results, behaviors.)

—What are we doing now that may be keeping us from reaching that alternative or goal?

—What are we not doing now that would make it possible for us to reach that goal? (What resources are available to help us?)

—Who will be responsible for our efforts to reach the goal? (Unfortunately, many problem-solving, goal-setting efforts stop just before this point, with no clearly defined assignment, or assumption, of responsibility.)

—What kind of a timetable are we using? (You need a schedule in order to know if you're making progress.)

Many people in problem-solving, goal-setting situations tend to restrict the number of options or answers available to them. They define the problem in unnecessarily narrow terms. As an illustration, suppose there are four assistants in a particular office. All have rather heavy workloads. One assistant falls ill and will be out for a considerable period of time. Many people facing that situation would think only about what is to be done with this person's work. A more constructive—admittedly, more complex—approach is to think in terms of what would be a desired and possible goal. The goal is to achieve x quantity of output. What resources are available? Should the workload be reorganized? For example, instead of getting a temporary assistant to fill in for the sick assistant, perhaps the work should be redistributed so that only the lesser skilled assignments would be given to the temporary. There are any number of alternatives, if the challenge is seen as an opportunity to define a new goal rather than just to correct a deficiency.

MAKING DECISIONS

Many of the pitfalls of problem-solving are present in decision making: too few options, inadequate development of alternatives, not establishing responsibility. Many decisions are made before they have to be made, without sufficient data and without anticipating the consequences of the decision. Some people pride themselves on their rapid decisions, confusing speed and decisiveness with good decision-making skills. What counts, of course, is not how fast you can come to a decision, but that your decision be a good one.

If you want to be an above-average decision-maker, the following guidelines can be helpful:

• Don't rush into a decision. The need for it may dwindle. Circumstances may change. You may get help you didn't know was there.

• Get everyone in the act—everyone, that is, who may have anything at all to do with the decision. If you need implementation by others, it is better if they have some involvement in the decision—and they won't unless they have participated in the process.

• Regard the follow-up period as being as important as the decision-making process itself. This is where a lot of slippage occurs, resulting in poorly executed decisions. People who were in on the decision need to be kept informed of the implementation, even if they are not directly responsible for it.

• Know how to reverse a bad decision. When things start going sour, when it looks as if you would do well to take the losses you have incurred rather than risk more by letting the decision stand, get objective counsel. The word of someone who is not emotionally involved in the decision can be very useful. If you decide to reverse, pull in the people who have been involved in making the decision and implementing it—as well as the people not directly involved but who might have been the beneficiaries—and tell them the facts. Make the announcement as quickly and as cleanly as possible. Try not to put the blame on a particular person unless there has been obvious, egregious wrongdoing that is public knowledge (or unless *you* are primarily to blame, in which case you'll have to decide how much to level with people).

• Finally, do not let anyone convince you that making decisions is a lonely business. There is plenty of help all around you. And most people are flattered to be asked to contribute. With more data and more specialized help, your chances of making a realistic decision are increased. And regardless of how much assistance you may have had, you still get the credit for having made the decision.

SPEAKING EFFECTIVELY

Most men and women are probably not aware of their patterns of speech. Women are frequently charged with having unpleasant speaking habits. It is also probable that the introduction of a woman's voice into what has been exclusively a male preserve may be disconcerting to some men. Many women who find themselves in a predominantly male environment clam up or speak in very hushed tones that no one can hear. Some management development sessions for women exclude males on the grounds that women often fade into the wallpaper if men are there; these women have to get used to the idea that they can talk up, that their contributions will be accepted.

Both men and women have to watch for irritating and distracting speech mannerisms. Many people mumble. Most people talk too fast when they're angry or excited and frequently their voices become higher-pitched, sometimes shrill. Observing the speech characteristics of others will give you a clue to your own mannerisms. It's also a good idea to make a recording of your voice, so you can hear how you sound to others. Your voice should be an asset to you. You have only to hear executives talk to realize how many of them have cultivated a pleasing, or at least a nonabrasive, manner of speaking.

When you are making a presentation before a group, irritating mannerisms and qualities of the voice are magnified. Here are some suggestions for making a group receptive to you and for getting your message across as clearly as possible:

• Develop an outline for your talk and rehearse with it several times (one or more times before someone else). Confidence in knowing what you want to say helps you to stay on the track, to be concise, and to keep your voice in the lower and more pleasing register. Uncertainty, anxiety, and fear generally make the voice rise in pitch.

• If your presentation is very technical, and if your audience is not on your level of sophistication, circle all technical terms and make sure you explain them. Consider using visual equipment and slides, bearing in mind that too much reliance on audio-visual equipment can put you in competition with it.

• Slow your normal rate of speech slightly—and think low (for lower register). Pause between sentences. Breathe as normally as possible.

• Speak to your audience. Some people when using slides or charts wind up talking to the visual material. Whenever you turn away from your audience while speaking, you can be sure someone is going to miss something in your message.

• Ask someone in the back of the room to signal you if your voice drops or you become less than perfectly clear.

• Speak to everyone in the group. Less skillful speakers tend to look over the heads of their audience, or to fasten on a friendly face and ignore everyone else, or to bury their heads in their notes, perhaps looking up occasionally. Eye contact aids substantially in getting your message across because it keeps people tuned in to you.

• If you start to ramble or otherwise sense you are losing control, stop. If you continue to talk, thinking that you will cover your problem, chances are you will only make it more obvious. So stop, consult your notes, or suggest that this might be a good time to take questions from the audience, or just ask, ''Am I going too fast?'' ''Is everyone with me?'' or ''Is there anything I've said that isn't clear?'' You will thereby gain a minute or so to recover and get back on the track.

THINKING CREATIVELY

Everyone is capable of being creative, to some extent. True, some people have larger veins of talent than others. Whatever potential you have for being innovative, you can develop it into a highly valuable skill.

To begin with, you need exposure to outside stimulation. There is no substitute for reading and discussing widely. Surprisingly in this day, when so many people in this country have had a higher education, comparatively few are serious readers. Most people do not read as many as a dozen books a year. Most do not read more than one newspaper a day, or two or three magazines a week. Much of the reading that you observe around you in your organization is predictable—and narrow: *The Wall Street Journal,* trade and professional journals, and perhaps *Fortune* or *Business Week* magazine. Many people will tell you they simply do not have time to read. For most people this is really a rationalization—they have never developed strong reading habits or the intellectual curiosity that forms the base of those habits. There are others who restrict their reading only to publications and books that will not threaten their view of themselves or their environment.

In most organizations the catholic reader enjoys at least an intellectual advantage over her colleagues. But she can also enjoy increased creativity. Every time an idea in print challenges you or raises your hackles, you have an opportunity to broaden your outlook and sharpen your mental processes—as long as you do not spend your mental energy finding ways to resist everything that might be new or contrary to the perceptions you are used to operating with.

The first recommendation, therefore, in improving your ability to think creatively is to enlarge your exposure to stimuli. The second is to look for similarities between what you read and what you already know. Many people try to spot dissimilarities, and when they find something that does not agree with their opinion, they close their minds to it. Almost nothing can get through. No doubt you have been exasperated by people who are always on the lookout for what is wrong with a new thought.

The creative person, on the other hand, is alert and open to relationships that she never saw before. For that is the essence of creativity—seeing and being able to work with relationships between people, ideas, and things that were not perceived formerly. The third recommendation is to ask yourself how deep or how superficial are the resemblances. And why are you interested in them? This is often the first step in adapting someone else's thinking or knowledge for yourself.

Another technique for spurring creativity is to let your mind do what it wishes—free-form thinking, or free association. This may not be easy for you, especially if, like many people, you are accustomed to thinking in very concrete terms. However, most people daydream or become distracted; suddenly they realize they are no longer thinking about what they had intended to think about, and indeed are way off the track without knowing how they got so far off. This is a good opportunity to understand how your mind makes

associations—and to encourage it to make more. From the realization that your mind has wandered, trace back each step in the dis-
traction until you reach the point of departure. Daydreams and fan-
tasies are regarded by some as unproductive and undesirable, but
they are legitimate functions of the mind working nonlogically.

The routine in your life provides you with countless opportunities
to question the way things are—and to find new ways of doing
these things, or of looking at them. For example, take any procedure that is part of your function in the organization and ask these
questions about it: Why is it done this way? Is this considered the
ideal way? Who considers it ideal? What makes it the best way?

Another approach is to envision an ideal of your own—ideal
procedure, conditions, behavior—and to work back from the ideal
to see what would be necessary to achieve it.

Finally (although we have barely scratched the surface), one
young manager we know claims that she expanded her ability to
deal with new ideas by changing her focus from ''Why should I
consider this?'' to ''Why shouldn't I consider this?'' Using that
approach, she finds the rationalizations a bit harder to come up
with.

WRITING WITH IMPACT

Writing is another skill that many people agonize over unnecessarily. There are a few basic techniques that will help almost anyone over the rough spots. For example, remember the rule of who,
what, where, when, why, and how.

> Supervisors are invited to a discussion of the Occupational Safety
> and Health Act Friday afternoon at 4:00 in the cafeteria. The discus-
> sion will be led by Alfred Miller of the Personnel Department. There
> will be opportunities for each supervisor to ask questions about the
> aspects of the law that pertain to his or her operation.

That's it—who is invited, what it is about, where, why, when,
and how it will take place.

Of course, the data aren't always so specific. There are letters, memos, and reports that the writer must shape herself. Here are some steps that can be useful in the development of a written report, article, letter, or memo:

• Do some free associating. Some professional writers like to spend several hours or days jotting down everything that comes to mind that seems even remotely related to the subject area. This is not the time to censor oneself—there'll be plenty of time for that later.

• From your notes, pick out the main points. What is the chief premise or the main theme that binds the others into a coherent whole? List them all in outline form.

• Put the main theme first. Some people like to build suspense by leading up to it; but what they often build is annoyance in the reader who keeps wondering what the point of it all is.

• Rank the subordinate and supporting points. Unless you have a weak case, chances are you will have many more than you need. Eliminate any item that is less cogent than the others or that simply reiterates a point made elsewhere. Explain each subordinate point and, where possible, provide examples to which the reader can readily relate.

• As early as possible, let the reader know why what you've written should be read. Simply explaining why you thought it important to put it down on paper is not always sufficient. It is advisable to sell the idea by showing how the reader will benefit from what you're setting forth. "I know that you have been thinking of creating a new staff position, and I thought I would explain my interest in the job and why I think I am qualified for it. Perhaps this will eliminate the need for you to go through the time and expense of recruiting outside."

Many nonprofessional writers think that the skill of writing lies in having such a great command of the language that one can start with the first sentence and chug along to the end without a pause. However, that's rarely the case, even with the most professional writers. Nearly all do several drafts before they're satisfied.

To start your rewrite, you have to change your viewpoint and assume the role of the reader instead of the author. You are about to pass judgment on what you have actually said, and you don't want to be confused by any recollection of what you intended to say.

If possible, let some time pass before you read over what you have written. First, read it for the overall effect. Does it convey the message you want it to convey? If there are unclear points, poorly worded phrases, or ideas that have been omitted, don't stop to make changes then and there. Simply put a mark or a notation in the margin and keep reading. When you've finished, go back and work on the details. If in this reading you discover embarrassing or inappropriate words or thoughts, excise them now.

EXPRESSING FEELINGS

Yes, expressing feelings is a skill—presumed by men to be instinctive in women. But that is another myth. Actually the male presumption puts a painful burden on most women: If a woman expresses her emotions in an open and healthy manner, she confirms the stereotype of the emotional woman. Many women, therefore, who cry more readily than men (and men should envy this ability in women) feel compelled to head straight for the privacy of their offices or the ladies' room when their eyes well up.

Perhaps eventually men will find it easier and more permissible to express their emotions and to experience the psychological release that accompanies crying. In the meantime women working their way upward through a male-dominated hierarchy will find it useful to develop ways to express their feelings effectively, but without posing a threat to those to whom they wish to make their feelings known.

It is very important to get feelings out in the open where they can be dealt with honestly and constructively. If you behave in a way that offends people, that behavior creates an obstacle between them and you. They may be able to continue to work with you, but they will have to suppress some of their negative feelings to do so. Unfortunately, those feelings will be expressed sooner or later in ways that are more or less veiled. Suppressed feelings don't go away; they surface in a different form. Perhaps during a meeting you were attending one person suddenly began to make sarcastic remarks about another or began to engage in an excessive opposition to the other person's ideas. Such behavior may have been an indication of a resentment or a hostility that has refused to stay buried.

To ease working relationships, it's a good idea to talk about your feelings with the persons concerned. You'll get rid of the tension you're feeling, and they'll learn things about their behavior that they didn't know before. Most people do not intentionally place obstacles in the way of dealing effectively with others. Occasionally you'll find that a person who is behaving unpleasantly toward you is unaware of doing it—and further, has no desire to do so. The important thing is to discuss the feelings and behavior without threatening the other person's self-esteem. Here are some general guidelines:

Put the feedback in terms of your perception. "I have a problem, and I'd like to discuss it with you"; "May I give you some feedback about how you come across to me?" "I'm having some negative feelings about some things you're doing"; "May I tell you how I feel about what you're doing?"

Ask for acceptance of your feelings; don't require agreement with them. You are, after all, an expert in your own feelings. The other person may not agree to having done anything to warrant your emotional reaction. But he or she cannot deny that you feel the way you do.

Describe the behavior you saw, not the attitude you assume was behind it. Behavior is apparent; you can only guess at the attitude. And that guessing will lead to argument. If you tell someone that you saw her scowl, she can respond that she was not feeling that way at the moment. But she cannot deny that you saw a scowl. However if you tell her that you are convinced she scowled because she dislikes you, you might argue all night about the motivation.

Don't be judgmental. Some people, playing amateur psychologist, put labels on the behavior of others. For example, they accuse others of being "defensive," "insecure," or of "projecting." It is better to describe the impact of the offensive behavior on you rather than to say what you think it represented in the other person. He is an expert on his motivations and feelings just as you are an expert on yours. Stick to areas in which your two expertises don't clash head-on.

Try not to embarrass the other person. If it is possible and convenient, arrange to give feedback in private. Your purpose is not to destroy him, just to alleviate an uncomfortable situation or to put an end to offensive behavior. Embarrassing the other person will not enhance his receptivity to your feedback.

LISTENING

Listening well is a skill. There are courses given on it. Many of these courses deal with improving one's ability to organize data received from others in the process of listening: the main point, supporting arguments, and so on. And part of the job of organization is to filter out data that are not relevant.

Unfortunately, listening techniques that are based on logical listening may encourage filtering out parts of the message that are not logically related but that are essential to the communication. People communicate nonverbally as well as verbally. In fact, body language has been the subject of some very successful and intriguing books. Although there is not much reliable scientific information on the meaning of body language—gestures, posture, facial expressions—any good listener knows how important it is to look as well as to listen in order to get the complete message. That's what makes listening different from just hearing sounds. Getting the meaning of those sounds is listening.

Good listening is not passive. It is active—and collaborative. Effective listening is designed to help speakers express what they want to say and what we want to hear. Many people regard conversation as a competition rather than a joint effort. To them it becomes a game of who can dominate the discussion. The role of listening should be passed back and forth—and usually is between equals.

Here are some other characteristics of effective listening:

Patience. This is the willingness to let other people have the time they need to express themselves adequately.

Openness. This could also be called *acceptance*. The listeners accept what the speakers say as being important to them. Acceptance is not the same as agreement.

Good timing. Active listening means responding. This encourages the speakers to continue. Responses are usually made to key statements, at the completion of a thought, or when the speakers indicate an openness to a response from the listeners.

Concern. The listeners invest themselves in what people are saying out of concern for them and what they think.

People frequently fall into the pitfall of hearing only what they want to hear. They want the speakers to talk about subjects they find interesting or to make statements they can readily agree with. If the speakers get into disagreeable topics, they may find themselves tuning them out. Listeners should therefore make an extra effort to be attentive when the topic turns to something they don't enjoy hearing.

Another problem many people have is that they judge the validity of the message by their feelings about the source. If the speakers are admired or revered, practically anything they say willl be accepted. If, on the other hand, the speakers are disliked for any reason, the listeners are unlikely to give much credence to what they say. Listeners should become aware of this error in judgment and guard against making it.

Keep in mind that listeners are valued highly by speakers because they show excellent judgment in listening to what the speakers regard as important. When those speakers are influential people who might help your career, it is to your advantage to listen well to what they say. And the bonus to all this is that good listeners often learn something of value themselves.

LEARNING

Much of what we have discussed about listening, problem-solving, decision making, and thinking creatively can contribute to more effective learning. On the negative side, many of us were never taught how to learn. We learned, but usually under duress: if you don't do this, you'll be punished.

Another drawback to the traditional education many of us were exposed to is that almost all of it took place in the classroom, quite removed from the environments in which we lived our "real" lives. Still another negative feature is that we spent a lot of time on subjects and facts that did not seem relevant to us. Thus, in terms of knowing how to learn effectively, most American adults today are disadvantaged.

While it is true that other people either through ignorance or perversity often make it more difficult for us to learn effectively, our own predispositions create obstacles for us. All of us have certain sets—patterns of behavior or perspectives. You may go to lunch every day at almost exactly the same time. There is one restaurant you refuse to go to because you vaguely remember having had an unpleasant experience there a long time ago. When driving, you react automatically to a red light. Women lunching with men are conditioned to let the men pay the bill. An administrative assistant in a large, prestigious corporation is sent to a division meeting in her boss's stead. Faced with a room full of men, she finds a seat in the corner and quietly takes notes, instead of taking the active role her boss would have taken.

A colleague of ours who has been a successful managing editor for a number of years perceives himself as unusually open to change. Yet during a recent editorial conference designed to encourage new thinking about one of the publications he was responsible for, he found to his amazement that he was arguing against all the suggestions—rejecting them automatically, without evaluation. This man was shocked to realize how strongly his sets were obstructing him and his associates.

Sets can be helpful, of course. It would be most burdensome and time-consuming to have to think through each thing we encounter as if we had never met it before. But those same sets can get in the way of new experiences, knowledge, and pleasures. It behooves anyone to challenge her sets occasionally as she recognizes them. Try that restaurant; take a different route to work; vary your lunch hour; read a newspaper columnist you disagree with.

Learning is important, and necessary for progress and growth.

But many of us learn so inefficiently that we risk losing options that could be helpful to our careers. Your learning methodology can be improved by (1) periodically challenging sets to avoid getting frozen in a resistant posture; (2) trying to relate what you are learning with your needs; (3) while learning, approximating as much as possible the environment in which you will apply the knowledge; and (4) seeking every reasonable opportunity to apply what you have learned, so that your learning will be confirmed and reinforced through successful application.

Much of current adult learning theory suggests that people learn more effectively when they feel it is to their advantage to learn. What I have to learn in this course (or seminar, or book) is something I shall have great fun learning. Or it will teach me to do something that I need to know how to do. Or there may be an external reward of a promotion, more money, or a better job elsewhere.

If your boss suggested that you take a short course on budgeting because it might come in handy some day, undoubtedly you would tend to consider the suggestion seriously, if only because the boss recommended it. Still, you would be preparing for a contingency that might never occur. It is likely that you would invest considerably more of yourself if the boss were to say, "I want you to take over the department's budgeting when you come back."

If you're in a potential learning situation but don't see the relevance of the subject matter, put the burden on the instructor to make it relevant—or to make it possible for you to do so. However, the burden is on you to let the instructor know there is a problem. Usually the instructor cares enough about the effectiveness of his teaching to welcome the suggestion.

Your learning will also be enhanced if it takes place in an environment and under conditions that closely resemble those in which you will have to apply the knowledge. If you take a course in the techniques of problem-solving, consider having sessions with people you work with and dealing with the problems you encounter on the work scene. In this way you not only solve the problems that hamper your effectiveness but you also work on relationships with the people who share your problems.

DEALING WITH SEXISM

In order to achieve interpersonal competence, the aspiring woman will have to be able to deal with sexism—prejudice directed at a woman chiefly because she is a woman. One sticky problem in overcoming sexism is that many men (and women) don't know when they're putting women down, and many women don't recognize that they're being put down (probably because they've been conditioned that this is their lot). Become sensitive to male put-downs of women. It is behavior that should be changed.

The ways of expressing sexism are almost infinite. Telling jokes in which women are treated as dumb or as sex objects, calling women "girls," having high regard for a woman primarily because of her anatomy, refusing to treat a woman as an individual or as equal to men—all such behavior perpetuates and reinforces the false notions that women are inferior to men, that it is a man's world—in which women have no significant place—and that women's usefulness is restricted to a relatively few subordinate roles.

The woman who wants to be successful in organizational life, to compete with men for the best positions, can ill afford to let the men she comes in contact with judge her according to the stereotype. Dealing with sexism, therefore, is a very important skill that women should develop.

Step one is to not sanction sexism. For example, don't laugh at jokes that demean women. The issue is not whether you are a good sport with a sense of humor but whether you are impelled to stand up for your dignity and equality.

Another example of sanctioning chauvinistic behavior is the tolerance women display when references are made to their anatomy—great legs, buxomness, revealing clothes. If a woman wishes to be seen as a sexy plaything, that's up to her. But as such she ought to realize that men may not take her seriously as an equal co-worker, a boss, an aspiring and worthy climber of the ladder. For many men, it is much easier to treat women in traditionally sex-oriented ways than to have to deal with them as full-fledged members of the organizational hierarchy. Everyone loses, of course, when women are put down. Women continue to suffer from the stereotype; men avoid having to develop constructive ways of working with women. And the organization loses out on important resources.

Step two is to develop ways to handle situations that involve sexist behavior without doing long-term damage to your career aspirations.

When you encounter a remark that you consider prejudicial, consider reacting in one of the following ways:

Ask for an explanation. This is a useful technique if the remark isn't clearly and unmistakably biased. As an illustration, suppose you are discussing a new job opening with some male colleagues. Several names are mentioned, all men. You submit the name of a female. One of your co-workers says, "Well, we can't very well promote her." Ask why. Or pretend not to understand. Make him explain the rationale behind his statement.

Don't be quick to charge discrimination. That usually will put a man on the defensive and force him to come up with all sorts of "valid" reasons why he is not sexist. Request that the person who made the remark explain what he meant. If necessary, persist—calmly but firmly. If you can keep him fishing for words and reasons long enough, you may not have to charge him with bias; it may dawn on him without your active help.

You can be direct without necessarily sounding bitter or hostile. For example: "Would you say that to a man?" "How would you like it if the women around here referred to you as a boy?" "Why do I have the feeling you said that because I'm a woman?"

There may be times when you feel justified in adopting a more militant and pointed response. One woman who felt publicly humiliated by things her boss said about her went home and stayed there until he called to apologize. Another woman said that when a man apologizes for using a profanity or obscenity in her presence, she replies using an even stronger word. With some men a "shock" technique like this might be very effective, but with other men a woman may find she has simply exchanged one bad situation for another. For example, after a woman has shown that she is not uncomfortable with salty talk, she may discover that some men refer to her as foul-mouthed. Or if a woman explodes in anger over a man's sexist action or comment, she may simply confirm in his mind the stereotype of the overly emotional woman.

Watch out for joking with men about the chauvinism you encounter. Possibly the only benefit to be derived from joking about bad behavior to men responsible for that behavior is that the woman feels relief. The men won't necessarily feel pressure to change. In fact, they may actually feel reinforced in their biased behavior by the fun it creates.

At the core of interpersonal competence is the ability to recognize that each situation is different from others and to deal with the differences. Thus, it's risky to try to develop generalized behavior that will be effective in all situations and with all people. However, we can offer some recommendations that will be applicable in most situations. Use firmness rather than hostility in rejecting unacceptable behavior; focus on the issue of sexism rather than on the person who is showing bias; respond immediately or as soon as possible to one incident instead of allowing many incidents to occur and your anger to build up over them; label the behavior as offensive to women and not as a personal insult to you (unless, of course, it is); be supportive and appreciative of men who are clearly trying to overcome the effects of their lifetime of sexist conditioning.

9

DEVELOPING YOUR BOSS AS A RESOURCE TO YOU

In the sophisticated climate that exists in most organizations today, in our increasingly mobile society, it is extremely unlikely that any woman could justly complain that her boss wrecked her career. There might be an isolated possibility of a woman feeling that her boss made her career. But there can be no doubt that a boss can be helpful to a subordinate's career progress; and that help can be especially valuable to a woman who is pioneering in a predominantly male hierarchy. It would however be presumptuous of a woman subordinate to expect a male boss, on his initiative, to make her upward progress speedier and easier. A harsh reality of organizational life is that no matter where you may be on the ladder, you need to look after your own career. A bit of altruism is admirable. But few climbers experience the kind of security that permits them to give substantial attention to those coming up behind them.

Occasionally the ambitious person will encounter genuine generosity from a superior, which derives from an appreciation of the subordinate's abilities and a recognition of the organization's needs for those abilities. But it is more realistic to accept the probability that an appreciation of a subordinate by a boss is less than altruistic. In fact, on both sides the attitude is likely to be: "What can she (or he) do to benefit my progress?"

WAYS YOUR BOSS CAN HELP

The relationship between you and your boss can and should be a mutually helpful contract. If you are fortunate to have such a contract, there are many ways in which your manager can have a potent constructive influence on your upward mobility.

Space to grow. Many subordinates are forced to operate within the limits or constraints imposed by their superiors. It is not unusual for a subordinate to have to conform to the boss's conception of the job. (And if the boss had the job before, it may now have less content, since he may have taken the most challenging part with him when he was promoted.) You are especially fortunate if you have a boss who is willing to let you—within reasonable limits—shape the job to *your* specifications and abilities.

Guidance. Your boss can knowledgeably observe your activity and give you feedback on your effectiveness, and can save you a lot of trial-and-error experimentation. Furthermore, your boss can alert you to the strengths he or she sees in you. Too often, people are more aware of their weakness and put too much effort into overcoming them and too little effort into building up their strengths. Having counsel available to you when you feel you need it is an advantage you will come to appreciate. In addition, your boss can keep you informed about the organization: the opportunities available, major changes in your department, and other developments.

Special assignments. Your manager can arrange for you to get assignments outside of your regular responsibilities, such as working on task forces and committees, either on your own or representing him. These temporary duties add to your experience and increase your visibility in the organization.

Public relations. You can benefit from having your boss blow your horn for you, especially if he has the ear of top management. The more your boss is willing to publicize you, the less time and energy you have to take away from your regular duties to do it yourself. And since you are on a lower level, you could not have the impact on the important people that a person who is closer to them can have.

Increased mobility. It is possible to move quite far up the promotional ladder with an ambitious, highly mobile boss. It may not always be to your advantage to stick *too* closely with your boss, but you may be able to do some moving ahead with him or her. Also, a mobile boss is likely to understand how important it is for you to get ahead. And even if you don't move with your boss, his or her mobility will create openings for someone—hopefully you.

Communications. The boss in the pipeline can serve your welfare by getting your ideas, suggestions, and proposals into the right hands outside the department, and by keeping you informed about what's going on with whom in the organization—the background information you seldom get through formal channels.

Protection. If you are the least bit nonconformist or innovative, deal informally across boundaries, or participate in joint projects, you may be subject to a great deal of sniping. Your boss can leave you out there to hang all by yourself (for his own protection), or he can absorb much of the impact himself, passing along to you the helpful feedback without all the poison. When you have a boss who is willing to take some of the shocks for you, you can use your energies for more constructive work.

Prestige. Working for an extraordinary executive can be most rewarding. If your boss is known to be very demanding, or is difficult and unpopular, people will admire you for your ability to deliver, for your tolerance, or for being able to do something they aren't certain *they* could do. If your boss is on a fast track, it will be assumed that you too are on a fast track.

These are some of the advantages you can enjoy with the right kind of boss. You will not be an automatic beneficiary; in most cases you'll have to pay the premium of being a reliable and supportive resource to him. But what your boss can do for you will be of special value to you. His efforts on your behalf and his support can speed your acceptance by others and can open the minds of other people who would not otherwise have been disposed to consider you as an equal.

Even with a boss who is both able and willing to contribute to your growth and development, you would be well advised to *design* that growth and development—as far as it is in your power to do so. No one else is as interested in your advancement as you are. No other person knows as much about you as you. And no one else has as much to lose if you neglect your cause or allow yourself to get sidetracked.

Next to you, the chief obstacle to your career progress can be your boss. You may find yourself behind a shelfsitter, a person whose progress has stopped. Unfortunately, while this person sits there, you probably won't go anywhere either. In this situation there may be certain reasons for continuing to work for this boss. For one thing, you may feel he has a great deal to teach you. Of course, you have to assess the quality of what you can learn from him; the organization has *some* reason for no longer promoting him.

Another reason for sticking with your boss is that you believe you will be promoted into his or her position. But this can be a trap. Most assurances about a future promotion are no more than speculation. Your boss may just stay in the same spot, or the job may get phased out or reorganized. At the last minute you might find yourself in competition with someone who has more powerful sponsors than you. Or someone may be hired for the job because the company assumes that no one inside is qualified to fill it.

A third reason why you might not be ready to make a move is that you're new to the position. You may need more time in it before you've gained enough experience to move on.

The difficulty lies in being able to recognize that a particular boss is not, and never will be, a substantial resource to you. This is chiefly a matter of discovering that the real action is going on somewhere else. Some clues: Your boss is not involved in the decision-making process but is informed of decisions made by others; you begin to hear disparaging remarks about him made by members of other departments; you get information as fast as your boss does, or faster; your boss shows few signs of desiring to move ahead and more concern about holding on to what he has.

You will probably be able to learn the most essential aspects of your job in one to three years. By the time that period has elapsed, you should be putting yourself on a strict timetable. If you cannot get a reasonable commitment from anyone that there is a step up from where you are, start looking elsewhere (if you are not already looking) for a position that is closer to the fast track.

WORKING FOR YOUR ADVANCEMENT

Most of the rest of this chapter is devoted to answering the following questions: During the time you are with a particular boss, how can you benefit most from the relationship? How can you learn and prepare yourself for advancement? How can you get an ever increasing piece of the action?

You may be fortunate enough to have a boss who is willing to let go of more and more responsibilities, because he is working on his boss to the same ends. You may also have a boss who is willing to let you do more and more because he is happier doing less and less. That is all right, as long as you recognize that once you've acquired the experience that is meaningful to you you must move on.

But it's more likely that you will have a boss who appreciates your ability and at the same time feels somewhat threatened. Your boss is ambivalent, at times wanting to help you grow, at other times drawing back and putting you in your place if you get too aggressive. Rationally your boss may regard your success as a personal tribute; but emotionally he may have moments of suspecting that you're too ambitious for your own good and therefore should be watched carefully.

Complementing Your Boss

One key to getting more of the action is to find ways to do things your boss does not do well—or does not like to do. You might call your list of such duties a "dirty-work list." You'll be doing many of these things without gaining much glory for yourself: If you do some tasks well, your superior will get credit for your good work. But since there are many things your boss can do to help further your career, you may find it advantageous to work out a tradeoff. You will help him look good if the favor is returned. (The terms of the tradeoff may have to be kept exclusively in your mind, however.)

Here are some possibilities for your list of dirty work:

1. Talking to people your boss doesn't like to talk to. They may be other managers, employees of other managers, customers, people in other agencies or companies, or even certain subordinates. If you hear your boss groaning about having to call so-and-so, suggest casually that you would be happy to make the call. Or ask, "Since you seem to be busy, would you like me to talk with him?"

2. Getting information. Your manager may have difficulty getting information that cannot be obtained through formal channels. Or there might be a situation in which he cannot afford to have it known that he is trying to dig up some facts. You may be better at tapping the grapevine, or at sleuthing and prowling, than he is.

3. Skills your boss lacks. If your boss comes to you and asks for ideas for a project, either because this kind of activity is not his forte or because he feels dull-witted that day, offer him your ideas. But present them in such a way that he can pass them along as his contribution. It may be tough on your ego, but it is something you can do to help your boss look good. And that cannot hurt you—unless it becomes a lifetime habit for the two of you.

4. Covering for your boss. Supplying the skills your superior lacks, as we suggested above, is a form of covering. That kind of activity usually doesn't raise moral questions. Neither does the covering you may be asked to do when he is distracted by personal problems—temporary financial difficulties, a domestic row, a child who has gotten into trouble with the law. These problems can take him away from the office at times, or can preoccupy him during work hours. He needs help and doesn't want others—his peers, his bosses—to know of the situation. It's the type of filling-in that you may be glad to do—and that your boss may be very appreciative of. (He may also be willing to do the same for you if the need arises.)

But there are some types of covering activities that present questions of ethics and honesty. For example, your boss is keeping a heart condition secret for fear that management will put him in a less responsible job or insist on his early retirement. To avoid heart strain, your boss has to take a lot of time off. Other such situations are the boss who has a drinking problem, or the boss who is having an affair that takes him away from the office during work hours.

In determining whether you should participate in the cover-up, consider the following questions:

Will your assistance boomerang? If your boss comes to feel that what he has been doing is wrong, will his judgment also extend to you? Or will your boss resent the fact that you have been of help in the weakness or wrongdoing? Will your boss feel that your knowing about that weakness or wrongdoing poses a threat to his security and that he must do something to eliminate that threat?

If your boss gets caught, will you suffer too? Suppose higher management discovers the truth, and your boss is demoted, transferred, or fired. It won't be hard for people to figure out that you have been doing some covering, and the people in power will hardly look at your cover-up as being in the best interest of the organization. Furthermore, if they feel embarrassed that your boss was getting away with something for so long, they may get rid of you because you remind them of their goof.

Does the cover-up require lying? There are lies, and there are lies. To say that your boss is attending a meeting away from the office when her son has gotten in trouble with the law and she is meeting with a lawyer is one thing. But to report that your boss is on a business trip to another city when she is on a three-day bender seems to be qualitatively different. Modifying the facts occasionally is not the same thing as a complete fabrication, especially when it may have to be repeated and embellished time and time again.

Will your boss's activities hurt the department? Are they illicit, or the result of weakness or incompetence? If so, they are likely to have an effect on employee attitudes and behavior. Can you, and do you want to, try to overcome these effects?

If, after honest and careful consideration of these questions, you conclude that, no matter how much you feel you owe your boss or how fond of him you are, you cannot risk the effectiveness of the department, the employees, and your long-range plans by offering your protection, you will have to tell your boss of your decision. He or she may not like it but may be able to understand your position. If, on the other hand, your boss threatens you or your career or promises that your relationship will become unpleasant or unbearable, seek counsel of a friend or neutral party. You may be advised to make a switch, and in fact an opportunity may be opened up for you. Above all, if you decide that the only solution is to go over your supervisor's head, be careful how you do it and be prepared for the possible consequences (getting fired).

Office mother. In addition to (or instead of) cover-up activities, your boss may encourage you to play another kind of protective role: "Keep that fellow away from me!" "Don't bother me with that kind of employee request!" "Look, if the vice president wants that kind of idiotic information, give it to him, just don't let him get me involved in such stupidity." (Male assistants get this kind of instruction too.) It can be dirty work, or you can turn it into an opportunity by getting your boss to delegate certain responsibilities to you. Unfortunately, if you play what appears to be a protective role, others will view you as maternal. And, in fact, your boss may want you to be his office mother. Often, women who have taken on this maternal role discover that men value them as confidantes, a sympathetic shoulder, a sounding board, but not as full-fledged, competent equals. If your boss wants your advice as a partner, fine. If he wants maternal comfort, consider letting him know at the outset that it is a role you are not very good at—and don't intend to improve in.

Office wife. The role of office wife is equally fruitless. Chances are your boss will expect complete loyalty and submissiveness—probably what he expects (and may or may not actually get) from his real wife. As an office and surrogate wife, yours will be an unequal partnership. You will be expected to provide him with support, to hold his hand, to absorb the abuse that he would like to but doesn't dare inflict on a peer or a superior. The boss who wants an office wife wants someone to relieve his loneliness, to pick up after him, to bolster his ego and confidence, to admire and revere him. It's a very demanding role—and nearly always an inferior one.

Surrogate daughter. There are bosses who view their secretaries or assistants, especially if they are younger, as surrogate daughters. The protective roles are reversed: the boss is the one who is protective. If you are cast in such a role, you may anticipate that your boss will wish to guard you against harsh realities. You probably won't receive any challenging assignments. Your boss may even monitor your organizational contacts: "It won't do you any good, my dear, to be seen with him (or her)." And when eventually you feel suffocated, your boss, as a doting father or mother, will be unlikely to welcome the idea that you want to get out. In fact, the seeming rejection may make your boss want to take revenge on you.

Assistant-lover. Last, but by no means least, there is the situation of the assistant-lover. The romantic implications in the male boss–female subordinate, or female boss–male subordinate, relationship are present especially if the two co-workers have a good working relationship on both formal and informal levels. But these affairs are frequently short-lived and infrequently an aid to one's career.

Socializing with the Boss

In his book *Male Chauvinism! How It Works,* Michael Korda has this to say about the perils of drinking with the boss after work: "When a man has finished whatever business he has to do, he can refuse the next drink and go home. A woman in similar circumstances may have to accept the onus of turning down a social invitation. If she refuses another drink and goes home, she may be making an enemy; if she accepts, she may be letting herself in for a torrent of autobiographical information or a pass." [1]

If a woman likes her boss as a person, if they have mutual interests, why shouldn't they have lunch together, a drink after work, or even dinner, for that matter?

Some women reply that there is a great deal of risk involved in any such relationship outside the office. For one thing, it may be blown out of proportion by company gossips who are always ferreting out what they think are interesting tidbits. For another, the woman may find her relationship with other people changing as the result of this social relationship with her boss.

Co-workers may resent the possibility that she will receive special treatment from her boss. Top management may disapprove of such outside relationships as a matter of company policy. Thus, a woman may run into problems when it comes to being promoted. (Her boss may also, of course, but any sanctions will undoubtedly fall harder on her.) And the final argument against the social relationship is that however innocent it may be at the start, in time it may lead to a complicated, even distressing, personal involvement that could threaten a woman's position in the organization and her private life as well.

It isn't always easy to turn down an invitation from one's boss. The refusal may be regarded as a personal putdown. And it can be even more difficult to turn down a series of invitations. But if you feel you should not accept an invitation of this kind—at this particular time or any other time (you know your boss is going through an unhappy period at home, for instance), you will need to be able to deal effectively with the situation. Here are some suggestions:

You can be busy. It isn't necessary to specify what you will be doing, although there are any number of plausible "excuses" you might use—a previous engagement, a night course, an appointment. And excuses of this kind can be used again and again, until the message is clear.

If you aren't certain that you want to make your turndown final, suggest to your boss that you'll take a raincheck—in the hope that next time the vibrations will be better, and safer.

You can refuse—now and for the foreseeable future. This calls for a long-term excuse. For example, you are interested in one particular man and he takes all of your spare time; you are needed at home to relieve your mother (sister, husband) of taking care of the family; you don't drink; and so on.

You can level with your boss. This can be touchy, since the male in question might be sensitive. But handled tactfully, it may be the best move of all. A good approach: "I enjoy working with you and talking with you in the office. But to see you after hours—I know it's innocent, but it just doesn't feel right."

And if your boss doesn't accept that gracious reply, you can at least take comfort in the knowledge that your decision to say no was the best one.

Now, what if you see no good reason not to occasionally go for a drink with your boss after work? You may be absolutely right. But even then, it's probably a good idea to impose certain conditions that will keep things on the safe side. For example:

Set a time limit. When you accept the invitation, tell your boss that you have another engagement elsewhere at, say, 6:30 p.m. That way, there is little chance that your boss will urge a continuation of the conversation over dinner.

Pick the place. This way you can be sure that you'll be in a convenient location when you're ready to leave, and that you won't be in a place that has the reputation of being a spot where co-workers who are romantically involved go.

Regulate the conversation. Most female employees have a fairly good idea of the topics they can safely talk to their bosses about— subjects of mutual interest that don't get into their personal lives and don't involve scurrilous office gossip. If a boss tends to wander off these subjects into potentially dangerous areas, you should tactfully get him back on the right track.

If the situation arises, or perhaps before, you will have to decide whether or not to socialize with your boss. Your decision should be based on frank consideration of the relationship you have with him, the relationship you want to have, and the changes that may occur in your career situation as a result of socializing or not socializing.

Keeping Your Boss from Error

One of the most important roles an assistant can play is to help her boss to avoid making errors. In an unsatisfactory, unhealthy boss-subordinate relationship, there is not only an observable lack of concern in the subordinate about the consequences of a mistake in judgment on the boss's part, there may even be a certain pleasure in the possibility that the error will bring humiliation on the boss.

If you find yourself enjoying or hoping for a mistake on your boss's part, you should reevaluate your relationship. Bear in mind that the boss's error may reflect poorly on the whole department. Thus, there is little to gain when a subordinate stands aside and lets the boss risk doing something foolish.

Even in the healthiest relationship, where there is a high level of trust and mutual respect, it may not be easy to tell the boss that he has fouled up or is about to. But easy or not, there are ways to call attention to a possible error that are constructive and tactful and that not only get the job of questioning done but can also make it a learning experience for you. The first step is to tell your boss that you are having a problem understanding him, not to suggest that he has made a mistake. You can easily and honestly say that the reason you don't understand why your boss arrived at this conclusion may be that he knows something you don't know.

Usually you don't rush to challenge a decision your boss has made. He or she may be wrong, but not so wrong that you want to make an issue of it. It's possible that he is merely carrying out a directive from someone higher up the line and may also feel a mistake is being made. If so, your suggestion that he is going along with a bad decision may not be welcomed—even if that is the case. You may jeopardize your previously good relationship if you put your boss on the spot in this way.

There are times, however, when you have to speak up. A challenge is necessary when:

• The mistake will hurt you. If the damage will be done in an area for which you are accountable, you must consider your career as well as your boss's. Further, there are people working for you who may be hurt.

• You are expected to help your boss look good. You really aren't doing your boss a service by not telling him that you feel a mistake is being made. And going along with a decision that you know is wrong is closely akin to what is called "malicious obedience." It won't benefit you—or your boss.

Once you've decided to challenge a decision, what's the most effective way to go about it? Here are points to consider:

• Can you be direct? Much depends on your relationship with your boss—and on your boss's character. Perhaps the last thing he wants to hear at this point is an objection from you about a decision he is already committed to. He might construe it as sheer obstinacy on your part or as a challenge to his authority.

To avoid such unpleasant reactions, you might ease into the discussion like this: "I keep thinking about how much that new machine costs. Prices have gone up so much that I was wondering if we might not be better off making do with the old machine for another year. Maybe you can explain why we should be getting it now."

However, if your relationship doesn't require this sort of roundabout approach, you can tell your boss directly but tactfully that you think the decision is wrong and why. If he is an effective executive, he will listen, even if he has heard the same arguments before.

• How much work are you prepared to do? Suppose your boss is about to, or has already, implemented the decision. Commitments may have been made, requisitions drawn up, funds allocated and accounted for. To reverse the decision will mean undoing a great deal of work. Your objections will have to be serious and well-documented, and your arguments will have to convince your boss and possibly higher management. Establish in your mind how committed you are to getting the decision reversed, and decide also on a point beyond which you won't push, a point at which no real gain will be realized by reversing the decision.

• How far are you prepared to go? It's usually not a good idea to confront your boss with the possibility (or the veiled hint) that you'll go over his head. There's little chance that such action will get you what you want.

It is worth remembering that a well-reasoned objection can often do more for your status with your boss than any number of agreements. And even if you don't win your argument, having had the courage to make it gives you a much better chance of being taken into the decision-making process next time.

Maintaining Contact with Your Boss

One of the dangers to an ongoing constructive working relationship is that the boss and the subordinate may lose touch with each other. It is ironic but true. People who have offices geographically close to each other, who communicate well, who have an excellent rapport will permit problems to occur in those communications. Both the boss and the subordinate can take too much for granted, assuming that the other is up to date on what is being done or is not concerned with the details. The subordinate has much to lose when this kind of communications gap occurs.

To prevent this from happening, you should drop in on your boss for an occasional chat. Granted there are some people who discourage casualness, but most do not. In fact, most people in organizations suffer from too little informal contact. There are many justifications for such contacts: something that has happened in the office, the political situation, something you have read, a movie you have seen, a conversation you know about or have had with someone else.

You should also discuss current problems. You don't need to have ironclad solutions, although it might be helpful, when you want to discuss a problem and its implications or want to tell your boss how your thinking is going at the present time. Give the boss room to contribute without implying that you want your problem solved for you.

If you have heard a rumor or seen some evidence that a decision has been made by higher management or in another department, seek information about it from your boss. This is not only flattering but opens the door to a useful exchange.

Go to your boss with suggestions. You may have observed that one of the secretaries seems ready for greater responsibilities, or that there is an unsafe condition in one of the corridors, or that a change in procedures or controls might eliminate an existing problem.

If you maintain regular, informal contact, you may succeed in encouraging your boss to reciprocate by visiting your office for casual discussions of work or other matters of interest to both of you.

Giving Your Boss Reinforcement

You can encourage certain kinds of behavior in your boss with positive feedback. Understandably, subordinates are sometimes reluctant to compliment or praise the boss. It may seem as if one is apple-polishing or currying favor. But giving positive feedback serves two vital functions. First, it lets your boss know he or she has been effective (and being the boss, there are probably too few people offering this information). Second, it encourages repetition of the kind of behavior that you found desirable.

So if you want to influence your boss's behavior in a positive, open way, be specific about what you approve of, give the compliment as soon after the action as possible, and be consistent—that is, let your boss know every time he or she does something significant that you approve of.

Talking About Yourself, Your Job, Your Career

You should from time to time initiate discussions with your boss about your feelings about what you are doing in your job. And you need to talk, for the sake of both of you, about your career orientation. Here are some points you should cover:

• Discuss your job content. It changes, sometimes without your being fully aware of those changes. You may discover that you are now doing more of certain kinds of tasks than you did formerly. Some tasks you never enjoyed before, probably because you were uncertain of their real importance or of your ability to do them. Now you may have found to your delight that not only do you do these kinds of tasks well, but you enjoy them. Perhaps you would like to do even more of them or perhaps you would like to return to doing other things that you once did more of. The job changes. Your abilities change. How you feel about what you do changes. And it is important that your boss know in order to correct imbalances, to assign new and greater responsibilities, and to stay informed of your growth and progress.

• Talk to your boss about your work relationships. There is nothing static about your relationships with employees, peers, your boss, and higher management. Many variables need to be explored. You need to assess those relationships and the significance of their changing dynamics. They can tell you much about your behavior, your competence, your strengths and weaknesses. Again, your boss needs to know how you are doing, and he will be able to give you counsel to help you build more constructive relationships.

• You and your boss need to compare notes on your learning needs. Some of your needs are related to the work you do now. You may have noted deficiencies in your ability to handle certain tasks. You may have settled on a plateau and you could use some new stimulation. Your boss will undoubtedly have data to add, based on observation of your performance. In addition, this is a logical opportunity to discuss your career direction and what preparation is desirable.

• You have a right to let your boss know what you expect. At appraisal time he evaluates how successful you have been in meeting his past expectations. At this same time, he should discuss with you his current expectations of you. You should take this opportunity to let him know what *your* expectations are for the period ahead. How specific you get with respect to the positive and negative influences he has on your performance and growth depends in large part on the degree of trust that has been established between you.

The discussion should be in the context of what you can do to help each other achieve your respective goals, not what you owe each other. The aim is a mutually supportive relationship that can materially enhance the progress of both of you toward your objectives.

If you keep your boss up to date on all these matters, you won't have the experience of one woman who worked in an office next to her boss, saw her boss almost daily, talked with her about as frequently, had lunch with her once every week or two, and then was startled and dismayed to find, in a discussion with her boss about her career plans, that the boss knew very little about her objectives. And what she did know was based on the woman's stated objectives of two years before, which were no longer valid.

Informal contacts between boss and subordinate are extremely important, but in discussing your job, your needs, and your career, make sure you supplement the informal discussions with those of a more formal nature. That is, ask your boss to set aside some time for you. Come prepared with notes. Supply a memo before the meeting or afterwards if you feel it will be helpful. The formality conveys a message that you consider the discussion very important. Casual conversations even about important subjects are rather easily displaced in the memory, and if they take place over drinks, they have a good chance of being forgotten—or very fuzzily remembered.

Respecting Your Boss's Turf

A story about a business tycoon demonstrates his brass and drive at an early age. During his hiring interview with a manager of the firm, he was asked, "What do you see yourself doing in five years?"

"In five years I see myself having your job," the young man is said to have replied. He was hired, and in less than five years he did have the interviewer's job. Obviously the manager who hired the young man either didn't believe him or had higher aspirations himself.

But many managers do not react this way. Your boss may not relish the idea of your planning to replace him when he moves on— since moving on does not always mean promotion. And your boss can hardly be blamed for finding distasteful certain things you do which constitute replacement while he is still in the job. If your boss is typical in his concern for his turf, you should guard against making decisions for him while he is away for brief periods, particularly if he is just away from his office but still in the building and returning shortly. For example, if there is a message for your boss, see that it is left on his desk, not yours.

There are other seemingly innocuous trespasses that assistants are guilty of. For example, an employee comes to you with a matter that should be discussed with the boss, but the employee says she doesn't feel she can be open with the boss; she would rather talk with you. You would be well advised to first get your superior's permission to handle the problem.

These examples may seem quite trivial—and objectively they are. But they can assume enormous significance to a boss who is less than perfectly secure in the presence of an ambitious subordinate. Of course, there are actions that a subordinate can take that are not trivial or innocuous, such as the situation in which an assistant, taking over for the boss during a lengthy absence, instituted some major changes and shuffled people around. The changes threw the returning boss into a furor.

Handling Conflict with Your Boss

Conflicts with your boss should in most cases be handled directly with him in private. It is bad form to carry on a lengthy dispute with your boss with other people in the department as observers or unwilling participants. A conflict between two people is difficult enough to work through; don't complicate it by bringing others into the situation. It's best dealt with in private, especially if one of you is likely to feel humiliated during the argument.

Going over the boss's head is very risky. Generally, his boss will feel obligated to support him. Recourse to higher management is very nearly a desperate step. You have to be prepared to take a few knocks from those you consult. They will probably not be happy about being dragged into the conflict; and they have a right to wonder why you and your boss have not been able to work things out.

Your best course of action when you have a problem with your boss is for the two of you to sit down together to discuss it as soon as possible. When you do this, be sure to stick with the issue or event. Describe what you saw happening or the disagreement as you understand it, and explain to your boss why you are disturbed. Don't be accusatory. Again, talk in terms of what you understand has happened. You should not attribute malicious motives to your boss. In fact, don't analyze your boss's behavior at all, if you can avoid it.

Describe your feelings; don't try to hide them. If you're angry, say so. Your boss cannot deny your feelings or your perceptions. Hopefully he will explain in what way his perceptions are different, which is an essential phase in working out the problem.

Persuade your boss that your primary objective is to reestablish a mutually constructive working relationship. You want to work with him and do a good job, and this conflict has gotten in the way of your effectiveness.

It isn't as simple as it sounds, of course. There may be strong feelings, resentment, suspicion. That's why it's so important to try to work through a conflict when it's in its early stages. If it goes on for long, a lot of emotions may get suppressed and issues confused, which will make resolving the conflict much more difficult.

The successful resolution of a conflict can do more than just remove an obstacle. It can give you valuable learning experience in working out interpersonal problems. And it can give you encouragement, when you see another conflict coming, to jump in and get it settled before it gets out of hand.

The Ideal Relationship

The issue of loyalty to your boss is not as clear as it once was. In previous generations it was assumed that you owed your boss loyalty by virtue of the fact that he was your boss. Today people are more likely to insist that loyalty should be reciprocal, a contract between two (or more) people. Actually, to some, the concept of loyalty is no longer very appropriate. A much more contemporary expression is *being supportive:* offering support and assistance to the boss's efforts to innovate, improve, advance, create—whatever he may do to benefit the organization, the department, the employees, outsiders who deal with the organization. Being supportive doesn't necessarily mean that you agree with everything the boss wants. What it does mean is that you support his efforts to do the kinds of things you feel are beneficial. You may take issue with some of the ideas but not with the offering of them.

But the question of loyalty these days is not restricted to how you relate to your boss. You are expected to be supportive to your colleagues, peers, and subordinates; observant of the objectives and policies of the organization; and loyal to the principles of your profession. These other ties can sometimes create conflicts in the boss-subordinate relationship.

The ideal relationship resembles a partnership, with the subordinate being the junior partner but growing toward equality. It is a collaborative, not a coercive, relationship—that is, subordinate and superior invest themselves voluntarily (not by command) in the achievement of organizational goals.

It is a supportive relationship, in which boss and subordinate each have an interest in the successful career of the other. The subordinate helps the boss look good in the eyes of his bosses. The boss guides the subordinate's attention to the appropriate opportunities and provides the means for her to acquire the skill and knowledge to advance. The boss also makes room for the subordinate to move around in, to experiment, even to risk making mistakes. The boss stands behind the erring subordinate, defending her right to make mistakes and learn from them.

The subordinate, through the acquisition of managerial ability, frees the boss to move ahead. The boss in turn acts as a sponsor for the subordinate, putting his prestige and reputation on the line for the subordinate who is worthy of advancement. If the boss cannot act as sponsor, he or she can at least make certain that the name of the subordinate is placed before the people making the decisions.

Obviously, achieving the ideal we have described here will be difficult, if not impossible. But the closer you get to it, the more you will profit from the knowledge and experience that a boss and a subordinate have to offer each other.

REFERENCE

1. Michael Korda, *Male Chauvinism! How It Works* (New York: Random House, 1973), p. 104.

10

BUILDING EFFECTIVE RELATIONSHIPS WITH PEERS

N EARLY all individuals who have meaningful positions in organizations have more responsibility than authority. That is, they are responsible for results, but they usually do not have authority over the people who must help to bring about those results. You probably don't have to look very far to discover colleagues in other functions or departments whose cooperation and good will you need to do a job. These colleagues can make your job difficult by giving you minimal cooperation—doing just what they have to do and no more—or they can make your job easier by offering you a great deal of cooperation.

We are reminded of a supervisor in a government installation whose responsibility was metal plating. When some metal arrived in his department from another, control over the other department's schedule came with it. If he didn't like the other supervisor, and if he could find the slightest irregularity in the paperwork that accompanied the metal, he would keep the work for a day or two and then send it back to the original department, insisting that the irregularity be corrected. But if he felt friendly toward a supervisor whose department had sent some work, he would take care of any irregularity over the telephone (or simply ask that someone come over to correct the papers).

There is a whole range of ways in which people in different functions and lines of authority can cooperate with each other. And, of course, cooperative relationships are by definition reciprocal—you should be willing to offer your peers the same information and assistance that they give you. Your peers can help you to learn more about the total operation, support you in your projects and your efforts to introduce constructive change, give your ideas and suggestions a valuable boost up the line to higher management, and even have a voice in your future progress in the organization. (Even though they do not actually make the selection, their recommendations regarding you and your performance will carry weight with those who do.) And if you do advance in your organization, some of your peers may become your subordinates. Clearly, it is to your advantage to start building good working relationships with your peers right away.

BREAKING INTO A GROUP

A person who has just been promoted or transferred into a group faces rather predictable problems. The new person does not "belong." The "ins," the other people who have been there for some time, know the group traditions, procedures, and relationships. It is not that the *ins* actively keep the newcomer out; they may simply not let her in—at least, not right away. Though technically (by title, function, and pay) the newcomer is part of the formal group, it may take some time before she is truly accepted as a member.

The informal organization (there may be more than one) is not, of course, on the organization chart. But it may be a force to be reckoned with. Such an organization may be no more than a group with a shared interest—people who like to go sailing together, go bowling, or have lunch together. Sometimes the interests are more work-related: the group may share certain values, such as ways of doing things, approaches to managing people, or a desire to preserve certain organizational traditions. An informal group may be protective—its members may feel that the organization is unconcerned with their welfare or is operating in ways that threaten their individuality. These groups exist throughout organizations, from the "rank and file" to the top managerial and professional levels. Despite individual differences, at any level the informal group satisfies certain social and personal needs, perhaps even power needs.

A female newcomer often faces an even tougher challenge than a male in gaining membership in both formal and informal groups. Here are some situations we have observed:

A woman was promoted to section head. One of the duties of section heads was to take care of calls from other departments and other agencies. Some male peers of this woman refused to acknowledge that she was the section head and insisted on talking to her boss, who would then take the calls, ask her for the information, and relay it to the callers.

A woman in her 30s was hired by a publishing firm as a managing editor. The other five managing editors were male. She found that her five male colleagues were accustomed to having lunch together, during which they often discussed business—and even made decisions. The woman was not invited to attend the luncheons, even though some of the decisions made at them involved her.

One woman was the first in her organization to be promoted into managerial ranks. And yet, three months after her promotion, a newly printed directory of managers omitted her name and title.

There are some general recommendations that we can offer to the woman who is trying to break into a formal, all-male group.

1. Ask for a position description. It is difficult for you to operate effectively without a description, although you may not get one without asking. If you can't get a description, ask your boss if he will have one prepared for you so the two of you can go over it together. Then go over the description with him. If the duties you

are performing differ from those formally specified in the description and from those performed by persons who hold the same job, ask your boss to explain the disparities. You may find that the disparities are not arbitrary, that you need to acquire more knowledge or skills in order for you to enjoy full parity with others who hold similar jobs. If they are arbitrary, based largely on the fact that you are a woman, then your forcing this discussion about them may be the first step toward parity.

2. If you feel excluded or discriminated against by the group, cultivate individual relationships. Drop into a man's office for a chat, ask questions, invite a male colleague to lunch. It takes time, but eventually there will be a sufficient number of men in the group who accept you as an equal and will protest any gathering or procedure that excludes you. In the meantime, of course, the individual men will probably be happy to keep you well informed.

3. Cultivate every resource you can. You may find that some of the female secretaries and assistants will be delighted to pass useful information to you that you might not receive through formal channels. You may also be able to develop some resources in other departments you deal with, people who find you efficient, pleasant, and generally satisfying to know.

4. Talk with your boss about specific difficulties. As an illustration, the female managing editor cited above found that her male colleagues had arranged an important meeting with the boss and neglected to inform her until after the session had started. She met with her boss later and suggested that a better communication system be established. You can also talk routinely with your boss about ways to achieve faster assimilation. Besides getting some good suggestions, you might succeed in making your boss understand that you have a special problem—and your boss could provide unique help. We do not advocate that you go in to your boss and complain, unless there has been a clear example of how your colleagues' prejudice has hampered your effectiveness.

5. Develop and exhibit competence. It may seem somewhat coldblooded to suggest that others will seek to establish a relationship with you if they see that it is in their interest to do so. The sooner you can show your male colleagues that you have expertise,

knowledge, and experience that can benefit them, the sooner they are likely to want to include you.

The informal groups may be an entirely different kind of challenge. At first you may find that the mere fact that you are a woman will cause you to be excluded from an all-male group. In time it may depend on what you have to offer—your strengths, your intelligence, the prestige of having you as a member—and of course what benefits the group can offer you. Membership in these groups may provide better informal communications, stronger support for your projects and ideas, more willing cooperation. Unfortunately some informal groups try to impose values on members that may run counter to those of the formal organization.

You cannot force your way into the informal organization. Nor can you insist that you are receiving unequal treatment (you can, but it won't do you any good). And generally your boss cannot help you, since by virtue of being the boss, he may also be excluded.

Your best bet may be to bide your time and to continue to demonstrate your competence, your willingness to work cooperatively with male colleagues, your high self-esteem that does not permit you to see yourself as anything but equal to the men, and your confidence in yourself that you are a worthy and full-fledged member of the group.

WORK GROUP SKILLS

A fact of life in any organization is "the meeting." And the higher you go, the more likely it is that increasing amounts of your time will be spent at conferences of one kind or another, formal and informal. One reason for more and more group discussions and decisions is that each individual cannot keep up to date on all of the developments in his or her field. Also, organizations are coming to be viewed more as systems, with changes occurring in one area having repercussions in others. Thus it is very risky for one person or one function to make unilateral decisions that may affect others.

Over the last decade there has been a growing emphasis on participatory management. Where possible, its proponents say, those who are affected by a decision should have some part in making it. It is not only that some of those affected may know more about the ins and outs of the decision—what it will involve and its consequences—than the people who have the formal authority to make the decision, but it is felt that a better job will be done if those who will have to implement a decision play some part in making it.

Yet, even though sitting in conference rooms takes up a lot of a person's time (too much, is the familiar complaint), there is in most organizations surprisingly little emphasis on the acquisition of conference skills by key people. Most meetings run far too long; too much unfinished business is carried from meeting to meeting; many meetings never seem to reach a clear objective (and indeed, some participants will admit that they don't always know what objective they're supposed to reach).

If you are looking for ways to be considered a hero by colleagues, to acquire some practical leadership experience, and to achieve some valuable visibility in the organization, one place you can start is in building those skills that will help you function effectively when you find yourself participating in a problem-solving or decision-making situation involving three or more people. There are three basic aspects of a group's functioning: content, methodology, and process. To be successful as a meeting leader and participant, you should be knowledgeable and adept in all three. Content, of course, deals with the subject matter the group is supposed to discuss and decide on. Methodology is how the group chooses to go about discussing and deciding on the content. Process involves the interactions among the people in the group. It is this aspect that most people find strange, uncomfortable, or controversial.

It would probably be helpful to further distinguish between methodology and process. If the group discusses how it will decide on certain actions (for example, by majority vote), that is methodology. But if some members point out that one participant seems bent on forcing a vote before the matter is adequately dealt with, which may affect the outcome, the group is moving into process.

There are several formal leadership functions, although in a truly effective group each member should be prepared to exercise any of them. Indeed, the most important formal leadership function may be to make sure that that leadership is shared by other members of the group.

Defining the problem. Most problem definitions are too narrow to permit the optimum range of choices. Peter Drucker has pointed out that one reason for the troubles of the American railroads was that they defined their problems only in terms of the *railroad* business. Had they considered the problems and opportunities of the *transportation* industry, they might have been able to deal more constructively with the competition that later crippled certain aspects of their business.

Part of the definition of the problem or objective is the explanation of any constraints that have been placed on the group's activities. For example, the accounting department's capabilities must be expanded, but only the space already available can be used; no new space can be leased.

Redefining or clarifying the problem. People who are deeply involved in discussing issues often lose sight of the original problem, making it necessary to restate it. On the other hand, the problem itself may change shape. For instance, the original problem may be that the accounting department's capabilities need to be increased. One solution is to increase them through a reorganization that will undoubtedly mean a shuffling about of responsibilities and supervision. The reassignment of responsibilities will necessitate changes not only within the department but in the way the department interfaces with other departments. This new dimension becomes part of the problem and must be stated as such.

Developing alternatives. Groups often show an inclination to settle early on one course of action. Evidence that groups are not as skillful in *generating* possible solutions as they are in *evaluating* solutions that have been developed and contributed by individuals may explain this tendency. Of course, a frequent phenomenon in groups is the power unit that has come prepared to push its preferred alternative. And in the early phase of group deliberation, the floundering-about period, this subgroup often succeeds in getting its way. For the sake of the effectiveness of the group, each member and especially the discussion leader must remain alert to the dangers of foreclosing options. The leader should encourage members to continue contributing ideas and to keep the discussion going.

Summarizing. Periodically the members of a group have to stop to assess what they have accomplished so far and the direction they seem to be heading in. The timing of this is important whether you are the formal leader of a meeting or a participant. A summary that comes too early in the deliberation can close out further exploration of alternatives; it can seem to indicate which direction the group should take. If too long a period elapses before a summary is provided, some members of the group may lose their orientation in the discussion. So much ground may have been covered that it will be nearly impossible to tie all the ends together in a summary.

Keeping the discussion relevant. It may also be a good idea to stop and summarize if the discussion has strayed off course. But if caught in time, it will usually be sufficient to simply ask, "Does anyone else feel that we've gotten off the subject?" It is better to ask the group if the discussion has strayed than to state that it has. First, an outright statement on your part can be interpreted as your trying to shut people off by suggesting that they have taken the deliberations out of bounds, which may make you the recipient of some unexpected denials and even unfriendly responses. Second, you may be the one who needs help in seeing how the current discussion *does* relate to the issue. And, third, if some members of the group are using the conference room to work out objectives of their own that have little to do with the group goals and are trying to neutralize your objection, you may need the support of other members of the group in order to get the discussion back on the right track.

Pushing for action. Many people engaged in various projects feel frustrated if a conference doesn't end with some kind of resolution. And yet, you will experience group participation in which there is no deliberate attempt to achieve a conclusion—or to make sure something results from the group's efforts. It sometimes takes courage to push for action, for closure, because the members of the group will probably be vaguely and uncomfortably aware that they have been sidestepping significant issues, anything, in fact, that might provoke open controversy. But when there is pressure to come to a resolution, the issues cannot easily be ignored and disagreements must be dealt with. You may be silently or openly applauded by other members of the group if you take the risk on yourself and press for some conclusive action.

Ensuring commitment. In too many groups the appearance of agreement is accepted gratefully. For that reason, taking steps to make sure that individual members of the group support the group's decision also takes courage—and persistence. Group commitment is especially important if there will be follow-up activity or implementation of the group decision. Group members who aren't committed may feel free to criticize the decision later, which will hardly contribute to organizational support for the work of the group. And if some members are expected to initiate or oversee the follow-up it is essential that they be committed to the group objectives.

Constructive Group Behaviors

There are certain additional activities that every member of a group—no matter how large, small, or informal it is—should be prepared to perform. You don't always need formal training in these activities. In fact, the best experience you can get is ongoing—in conferences of all kinds. You may not always function at top effectiveness, but you will be surprised at the encouragement you get from others—and their feedback will help you to sharpen your group skills.

Let us review some important and constructive group behaviors:

Encouraging. It is not easy for some people, especially those who see themselves as less powerful or less valued in the hierarchy, to express their views. Many people find it hard to speak out in public. That is why, when you smile and express your interest in what they have to say, you serve the group interests and earn the appreciation not only of those who are hesitant but of others who know that you will be equally encouraging when they make a contribution. You don't have to agree with what is offered; you just have to let people know you believe it should be put before the group.

Mediating. This is one of the subtlest and trickiest roles to be performed. Often in a group you will see a member jump in at the slightest sign of conflict in order to head it off. Such peacekeeping compulsions quash progress, although they may save people from discomfort and embarrassment. Obviously, people who disagree do not have to have a negative and disruptive influence on the proceedings. However, a conflict can grow to the point where people become polarized around the issues and even unable to hear what others are saying. The mediator steps in and asks permission to summarize and interpret the disputants' positions and also asks them if her interpretations are correct. Then she might make the following suggestion: ''Well, I think both points warrant more discussion, and I'd be interested to hear how others feel about what you two have expressed.''

Mediating has the dual function of relieving pressure that has become difficult to tolerate and of opening up the way to fuller participation in the issue in order to arrive at an agreement.

Harmonizing. This deals with finding areas of agreement. When a potential conflict develops, many people get very interested in defining the areas of *dis*agreement. It is not uncommon for two members of a group to express essentially the same concept using different terminology; yet someone can be expected to call attention to the gaps between the statements. If the areas of agreement are not pointed out, an unnecessary dispute with resultant polarization may arise.

Initiating. Introducing ideas or proposals is definitely a risk-taking venture. But it has its rewards, too. It earns points with co-workers, especially if there is a prolonged discussion of the contribution. If the idea is accepted, you will get some credit for it. In time, people may come to regard you as an innovator.

Listening. This skill, discussed in detail in Chapter 8, is very helpful in a group situation, because the person who has been listening can best perform some of the other roles we have discussed—summarizing, mediating, harmonizing, and so on.

Providing methodology. When the discussion bogs down on one or more issues, it is a good time to introduce some methodology, such as suggesting that the discussion stop and a vote be taken on one of the principal points to see where the group stands and where it ought to go from there.

There are, of course, a number of other constructive roles to be taken in a group. And there are relatively few people who perform them conscientiously, consistently, and skillfully. If you want to be noticed and to eliminate some of the anger of people who feel they spend altogether too much time in meetings, developing and perfecting your group skills seems to be a surefire proposition.

Obstructive Group Behaviors

We have already indicated some kinds of obstructive behavior that should be discouraged. Members of the group usually make it very clear to a person manifesting unhelpful behavior that such actions are not acceptable. Another of these behaviors is *blocking*. For example, the conference jester uses a fast funny line to short-circuit the impact that another member is having on the group. Or A is a slow thinker who does not arouse admiration in B. B fidgets while A stumbles along, and then interrupts to take the meeting in a different direction. Everyone now and then can be expected to block someone else, but if it is a pattern, it should be pointed out.

Judging another's behavior, as mentioned earlier, is to be avoided. If another person has angered or irritated you, you have every right to tell the person how you feel. You do not have the right to suggest that the offensive remark was based on his or her defensiveness, insecurity, or projection. It is an effective way to divert the group from its proper track while the two of you argue over whether your analysis of the other's behavior is correct.

A common activity in a group is *dominating*. It is not necessarily undesirable. But some people have such strong leadership needs that they must call all the plays. These people can wrest the actual leadership from the chairperson, stifle opposition, and subvert the group to their own ends. However, put to proper use, their talent for leadership may be an asset to the group. It should be impressed on those who attempt to completely dominate the conference that such behavior is not acceptable and that only constructive methods of participation will be used.

Contributing More Effectively in a Group

When speaking in a group, don't direct everything you're saying to one person's face. It's natural to do this when one person in the group looks as if she agrees with you, especially if she has a high profile. But if you talk to her to the exclusion of others, you not only will risk alienating others but will erode her effectiveness in supporting you—because you have helped to isolate her.

When your position is attacked, your first reaction may be to answer the objections as quickly as you can. But if you take your time, you may find yourself being defended by others in the group (and their defense may carry more weight than yours). You will also project a sense of security that will win admiration for you. Remember to listen carefully to objections. Even negative responses are valuable, since they give you feedback on areas in which you have not been fully effective.

Check with the group periodically to be certain you're making yourself clear. In case there has been a misunderstanding, assume that it is you who have not been clear; the others will not appreciate your suggesting that they have been deficient in listening or understanding.

If you meet with heavy opposition from one person and you begin to get bogged down, suggest that you backtrack to try to discover where you and your opponent agree. If you get hemmed in by an attack from more than one person, ask the group for help. "Do all of you feel this way?" "Should I just forget my idea?" "I guess I'm not doing such a good job explaining myself. Can anyone else help me out?" You might be surprised by the help you get. Of course, you must be prepared to be told that you ought to forget the whole thing; but even that is better than prolonging the agony.

Many factors that contribute to effective group behavior are really based on common sense and courtesy. Bear in mind that staying committed to your long-term goals in a group—to push your project, to win the respect of your colleagues, to achieve visibility and the reputation of a skilled organization person—will help you to build and maintain behavior that is congruent with those goals.

COMMUNICATING WITH YOUR PEERS

In most organizations, horizontal communications—between functions or departments that are in different lines of authority—are not as strong as they should be. Even though your chain of command is different from a co-worker's down the hall, it may be necessary for you and this colleague to achieve a constructive working relationship. And in the process, there are bound to be problems. So weak are the horizontal lines in some organizations, and so strong the discouragement to cross lines of authority, that some of these problems never get solved. Instead, they become accepted as the norm and create even stronger barriers to effective cooperation.

Operating Informally Across Boundaries

In your own efforts to improve collaboration with other managers and to work out problems together, consider these suggestions:

Let everyone have a chance to define the problem. When another department is involved, the odds are that you don't know all the factors in the situation, even if you think you do. It is most important, therefore, that those involved be allowed to describe the problem from their own viewpoints. You will often find that people differ widely in their conceptions of what a particular department's, or individual's, responsibility is. Unless these differences are expressed and understood, the group can never speak a common language.

Another reason for letting others define the problem as they see it is that problems—or at least their importance to the complainer—often disappear once they are given a full airing. The fact may be that they have become problems simply because the person who nursed them did not feel he or she could get a hearing. Once the problem is aired, it may not seem so important. By clearing away this underbrush of grievances, you can free the group to get down to the basics of the real problem.

Don't be thin-skinned. In any interdepartmental dialogue, some suggestions or solutions will not be entirely to your liking—especially if they seem to imply criticism. But don't yield to the urge to jump in and defend yourself against alternative answers which you may already have decided are unsuitable. The other managers are probably just as anxious to get to the truth as you are, and not as eager to embarrass you as you might be tempted to think. Sit back and let the suggested solutions be presented and examined. Your lack of defensiveness will point the way to a more objective evaluation. It is also important to offer your own suggestions as inoffensively as possible. Asking, rather than telling, is often the best way to do this.

Don't be in a hurry. Too many managers enter an interdepartmental conference with the assumption that everything can be cleared up in one session. They become frustrated when matters that seem to be extraneous are brought up, and the problem seems to move away from a solution rather than toward it. But the problem as any one person sees it is probably just the tip of the iceberg. When different perspectives are brought to bear, the problem is likely to grow rather than diminish.

A first meeting can be rated extremely successful if the participants can agree on what the critical issues are and what should be explored further. After all, if the solution were really simple and obvious, it probably wouldn't be necessary to have the meeting in the first place.

Prior to the meeting, it's very difficult to think through the situation as you believe another manager sees it. Therefore, his or her behavior at the meeting may puzzle and annoy you. Don't forget, though, that the other manager's behavior may be just as justified as yours. Undoubtedly, you both will have to do some compromising before the matter is settled.

Avoid being judgmental or accusatory. The two of you share a problem. Saying, "Your people are causing mine to have problems," only arouses defenses. Instead, acknowledge that there are certain procedures that are not going as well as they might. There is no need to assign blame. Even if the two of you decided that it was the fault of neither, that would mean finding a scapegoat somewhere else. And it is unlikely that progress would be made.

Decide what you want. As discussed earlier, a goal should be set that will provide improvements for both of you. Asking the question "What would be a better way of doing things than the one we have now?" is a starter. Think in terms of desirable alternatives.

Establish a responsibility and a timetable for improvement. Make sure that everyone leaves the meeting aware of who is to do what within what time period. A meeting should not be adjourned until these details are agreed on.

Tell your boss what steps you have taken. Not only does courtesy demand it, but you may later need your bosses as resources. For example, they may have additional information to contribute to the solution of a problem. Or you may have to call on them later to deal with higher management for you.

Developing Your Own Network

Solving problems is a small part of operating across boundaries. You can set up an extensive communication network for yourself that will probably beat the formal communication channels for speed and accuracy or at least completeness. In every organization there are people who always seem to know what is going on. They are valued as sources of information, which is something you might wish to think about if you are still trying to break into a male-dominated group. If you've come up through the organization, keep your old channels as open as possible for as long as you can. The mistake many upwardly mobile people make is that, for reasons of status, they cut off many of their old contacts as they go up. When they do this they lose valuable sources of information.

If you are going to cultivate other people as communication channels, you have to be prepared to give information yourself. And you have to know when to *keep* things to yourself if you want to maintain the trust of the people who give you information.

With respect to building trust, you must protect your sources. You may repeat some of what you hear, but you may not, even if cornered, identify your sources of information. Be casual and natural. Making a big production out of seeking information suggests that you want to relay it to someone else or use it in some way. Be selective about your confidences. People who pass information along to you want to be assured that you are discreet and trustworthy. Never use information against its source. Do not foster friendships or play up to people just because you want information. Keeping channels open means being friendly and sociable even when there is no gain to you. Of course, there are occasions when you go to a source and tell the person exactly what you would like to know. This can be flattering and effective, because you acknowledge that the person is in the know, and most people not only want to be in the know but want others to be aware that they are.

Of course, some people think that gathering information, even harmless gossip, *isn't* the dignified thing to do. But the people who get ahead in most organizations are those who have placed a high value on knowing what is going on—not just who is being considered for promotion, but why; not just that a certain multi-million-dollar order was mysteriously canceled, but why. Those who stay in their offices and wait for the information to come to them are often the last to know. Remember also that people who place a high value on knowing what's going on and who's getting ahead place a high value on subordinates who also like to be in the know. A knowledgeable subordinate who can supplement a boss's own sources of information is an asset.

PUTTING THE PRESSURE ON A COLLEAGUE

A prime breeding ground for conflict exists when two colleagues are working together and one doesn't want to cooperate or can't hold up his end. If you are the one being imposed on, you have to find a way to get what you need from your partner without permitting a conflict to develop that will delay the work or make its completion impossible.

Putting pressure on someone is not pleasant, and many managers shy away from doing it as much as they possibly can. But when two people are working together, each one of them with different problems and different responsibilities, their priorities may differ slightly—or extensively. When this happens, the manager who is committed to completing his own assignments may have to hound someone else. The problem is not whether or not to badger—but how to do it most effectively, and with the least unpleasantness.

What's the right approach to take in order to get action from a stalemated colleague (or even a boss or subordinate) without rubbing him the wrong way?

Don't apologize for hounding. An apology immediately puts you in a defensive rather than offensive position. And apologizing for putting on the pressure labels what you are doing and immediately puts the other person on guard. People do not like being harassed or needled, regardless of how much you apologize for doing it.

Don't make it sound like pressure. As much as possible make your request seem like a fresh one. You may have to refer to previous conversations, but give your present one its own reason; don't make it sound like just another follow-up. Think of a new contingency or angle on which you can base your approach.

Ask the individual when the work will be completed. Say that you're bringing up the matter because of your own time pressures. Explain why you need action on it, and ask the person to set a specific completion date.

Don't point blame. Show sympathy for your colleague's problems, and understanding of his reasons for not getting to the matter before this. Indicate that you appreciate his good faith in trying to get to your case, considering all the pressures he's under. Agree that it's rough—but stay firm in your own needs.

Don't personalize your request. Even if the matter is a personal one, it will usually involve questions of policy and protocol. Emphasize the need to iron these out for everyone's good. The more you depersonalize your demand, the less risk you run of doing battle. If it's at all possible, therefore, try to sell the individual on taking action because of the benefits that will accrue to him (or to his department).

Don't just load the assignment or task on the staller. Ask if there is anything you can do to help get it done. The more you contribute, the more certain you will be of getting what you need—when you need it. Even if there is nothing you can do to expedite the matter, the fact that you volunteered to help will keep your colleague from feeling that you're simply dumping more and more work on him.

Don't end the discussion without a commitment. If you do, you are just asking for another session, when you'll have to exert more pressure. Also, if you don't get some of your questions answered, you're just going to create more frustration for yourself—and chances are you already have more than enough.

If, after discussing the problem with your colleague, you find that it has become impossible to do what you set out to do, get your colleague's agreement to a new schedule, to modifications in the method, to changes in the people assigned, to a redefinition of the objectives.

When you feel you have reached an agreement, restate the terms. "Okay. As I see it, you and I have a contract that we will do x work by x date." Of course, a psychological contract isn't binding in a legal sense, but many people feel such a contract is ethically and professionally binding.

If your colleague seems hesitant at this point, offer to set new conditions or to renegotiate. This is the time to do it—not later, when the anxiety, frustration, and unfriendliness will be even higher. It is also possible that by patiently and amicably pursuing the commitment, you may stumble on a reason for delay or non-cooperation that has not yet been revealed. It is better to know that reason now, when you can still make some alterations.

CONTROLLING CONFLICT WHEN IT INVOLVES YOU

People involved in even the smallest conflict have a tendency to try to win minor battles, regardless of whether such victories really contribute to winning the war. It's difficult, of course, to monitor your own behavior, to note what you are doing as you do it, especially when you are under pressure. As a result, you may be sidetracked by minor points and lose sight of your real goals.

When there are important objectives at stake, therefore, it's a good idea to try to increase your awareness of what you are doing—at least during moments that are critical.

Try to anticipate things that may throw you off the track. You can probably recall words, actions, or attitudes that have thrown you in the past. Undoubtedly, there are certain people who can rattle or intimidate you more easily than others can. If you prepare yourself for these reactions, you may be able to lessen their impact and maintain your cool. This is especially important when you are seriously committed to a particular project, task, or objective. The deeper that commitment, the more susceptible you are to interpreting words, actions, and attitudes as an attack.

When objections are raised, don't leap into battle. Consider an experienced saleswoman's advice on handling verbal obstacles and objections: "I just sit there and nod my head, then I go right on with what I meant to say. I figure I don't have to stop to take care of an objection which probably isn't the real objection anyway."

The point is that attacks on your position don't have to be repelled immediately. Relax, listen, and persist in your line of reasoning. If your opponents feel strongly, they will interrupt again with a demand to be heard. When you are ready to answer, the objection will be waiting for you. Don't rush.

Watch for signs that you're rattled. When someone voices opposition to your thoughts and ideas, you may feel that you have to put your critic down. But face the facts. Can you afford to sacrifice the accomplishment of your original objective for instant, personal gratification? You probably can't. When you feel your face becoming flushed or your heart pounding and your palms wet, it's time to slow down and assess the direction in which the discussion is going.

Dealing with a Shouter

At one time or another, you have probably been the victim of a verbal assault by an angry colleague. Regardless of whether you had done anything to provoke the outburst, the experience was probably painful—and embarrassing if witnessed by others, especially employees who report to you.

One of the problems in dealing with a shouter is that even when you know the complaint is legitimate, you may get angry because you feel that the abuse is disproportionate to the seriousness of the offense. The validity of the complaint becomes secondary to the embarrassment this person causes you. Consequently, you may be tempted to respond with some angry words of your own.

In some situations a hostile response to a hostile attack may work. Many times it does not. The "attacker" may see himself or herself in a superior position—economically, socially, managerially—and thus feel justified in chastising you without regard to who may overhear. A hostile response from you may quiet the attacker or it may fan the flames even higher.

There isn't any one right way to respond to a verbal attack. But one approach that often works is to concentrate on stopping the attack, rather than responding to the argument. Your feelings are involved, and the experience is painful. Also, you want to stop the shouting. Probably the best way to do this is to meet feeling with feeling. But your feelings can be expressed in a controlled way. Here are some possible replies: "Please don't shout at me" (delivered in a low, earnest tone). "I know you're upset. Let's talk things over privately—without the witnesses." Or: "Look, I'm sorry you're so upset. When you stop shouting, I'd like a chance to work this out with you. I think we can settle it."

You can arrange to work out the problem or misunderstanding then or later. Your first objective is to stop the embarrassing spectacle.

Public shouting scenes are disruptive and embarrassing. Witnesses will usually be distressed by a prolonged show of emotion, even if they think the angry tirade is justified. Therefore, people who keep their cool under a fiery and withering attack usually command the respect—no matter how grudging—of those witnesses. But "victims" who seek to gain sympathy after the verbal attack often garner a harvest of contempt instead.

In short, this is one situation in which you will fare best if you resist the temptation to give as good as you get and try to defuse the emotionality of the situation to the point where you can discuss reasonably—and privately—what you did or didn't do wrong.

Conflict Resolution

One often finds in organizations certain myths about conflict. For example, there is the misconception that people really do not like conflict and will avoid it if they can. This isn't always true; for some people, conflict serves a purpose. It draws attention, and it can be embarrassing—hopefully to the other person. It can also be a way of testing one's strength in the organization. Another misunderstanding of the nature of conflict is the idea that it can be resolved through reason. Logic seldom plays a part in starting a conflict or in stopping it.

The aspiring woman, facing a conflict situation and partisan pressure on her, should try to act in such a way as to keep the confidence and respect of all disputants while avoiding traps that could inhibit her career advancement.

To this end, you should avoid becoming the group mediator. It's all right on occasion, but on a full-time basis it's a thankless role. Since you are a colleague, you are not likely to be trusted completely by either side. What you can do is offer to get an outside person who has no stake in which side wins the conflict.

Don't discuss the political tug of war with your subordinates. It can distract them from the business of running the department. And anything you tell them is likely to be passed on. You could thus find yourself unwittingly in the middle of the feud.

You may be asked by one party in the conflict to give messages to another party. If you agree to this, you will soon find yourself conveying the kind of information (and often misinformation) that is part of a win strategy. You will no doubt discover that you haven't helped to settle the conflict, but you may have helped to prolong it.

Of course, you will have to continue running your operation while the conflict is going on and, hopefully, being solved. If you interface with any of the disputing groups in the line of work, make sure that the people who report to you understand that you'll be judging them on how well they get things done even in the combat zone. But also determine as far as possible what benefits there might be for you in the resolution of the dispute. For example, if one side wants to merge your operation with another that you already work with but over which you now have no authority (but would after reorganization), that could be a plus for you. Whatever benefits you find, keep them in mind as aspects of the conflict you could endorse, if you are forced to take sides.

If you have to take a stand, endorse the issues and not the people representing them. Personal loyalty buys only so much—probably not as much as it once did in organizations. The important thing is for you to act in your own interest. It would be naive to assume the others are not acting in theirs. Figure out who has the power—or is closer to it. It will be to your advantage to side with the power. And be sure you say the same thing to all sides. No one should be able to accuse you of playing a deceptive game.

Keep in mind that there will be a post-conflict period. You will have to live with the disputants, which will, of course, be much easier if you haven't alienated anyone during the conflict. It is also realistic to assume that even though the conflict may be resolved, the disputants won't necessarily like each other. If you don't expect warm, friendly feelings, you won't be disappointed. One important and constructive role you can play during the post-conflict period is to accept the resolution and not to encourage any reminiscing or gloating by one side or the other.

Of course, this is all ideal advice. There will be times when you'll see direct and substantial advantages to you in jumping right in. And there may be issues that your conscience will not let you ignore. But, in general, avoid taking a stand for as long as you can. Endorse an issue rather than a person (the issue can't be fired). Go with the power if you can. And if you have to take a risk, try to make sure that there is a reward that could make it worthwhile.

Conflict—and political maneuvers—are inescapable facts of life in any organization. Your only options may seem to be staying out of it or getting into it. You cannot very well stay out of it if there are people and issues that concern you. But you don't have to rush to lay your head on someone's execution block either.

COMPETITION

We should say a few words here about competition, which seems so highly honored in American life. When the management of one company opened up its assessment center to women for the first time, some "women only" sessions were scheduled beforehand to help women get used to the idea of working competitively with men. There have been numerous complaints, especially from feminist consultants who work with organizations, that women are not sufficiently competitive—or assertive, a term that has been used as a substitute. Many people say that competitiveness is more characteristic of males than of females. It is certainly true that business organizations are often depicted, in the media as well as in fiction, as fiercely political and competitive.

Competitiveness has certain advantages: it adds excitement to a venture; it can enhance the learning process by creating an additional value for the learner; it can increase the cohesiveness of a work group that perceives itself in competition with others. However, too much competitiveness can help to create a win or lose attitude ("If I win, you must lose"). People who feel they must compete with one another may not be able to work together profitably—they may become more interested in "winning" than in achieving what is best for the organization. High competitive people eventually find it difficult to build trusting, supportive relationships with peers.

The woman who assumes a responsible position in an organization is not necessarily handicapped if she is not a fiercely competitive person. Many males have been conditioned to believe that winning over someone else is vitally important. If a woman has been fortunate enough to escape this conditioning, she can put the energy that others expend in competition to work in shaping her career goals and in acquiring the necessary skills to achieve those objectives.

II

YOU, THE MANAGER

Y<small>OUR</small> subordinates can be a rich resource to you in your career advancement. Yet their role sometimes gets overlooked or forgotten by the manager on a fast track. In fact, you will meet managers who view their subordinates as antagonists who must be pushed, driven, controlled, monitored, and manipulated if the job is to get done. Others enter into competition with subordinates, as if they must prove to themselves and to the world that they are superior to the people on lower levels of the hierarchy. Still other managers distrust employees for having the capability of embarrassing them, frustrating them, informing on them, or doing them out of their job.

The manager plays a key part in fostering a growth climate for those who have the will and ability to get ahead. A woman who has been subjected to discrimination in her own attempts to get ahead should be able to understand the needs, goals, aspirations, and feelings of her individual subordinates. Chances are that her own goals and needs have at times received low priority because she was seen not as an individual but as one of a group—women. Therefore she ought to be especially aware of how important it is to relate to employees on a one-to-one basis as much as possible, instead of treating them as members of a group. A manager should bring employees into the decision-making process when those decisions affect their welfare. She or he should evaluate them on the basis of their capability and competence in their work, not on superficial characteristics of looks, sex appeal, compliance, and fulfillment of a stereotyped role—as women have often been judged.

The enlightened manager today should try to avoid classifying and categorizing people, even though it's become fashionable in recent years (aided and abetted, no doubt, by the various psychological and sociological labels that have been devised). Many people are more comfortable dealing with labels and categories than with individual human beings. Whatever else the entrance of women into responsible organizational positions brings, this should be preeminent: the realization that it is unrealistic to deal with people as groups and to treat all members of a group the same way.

Complex though it may be, the ability to deal with *individuals,* rather than just with groups, is the mark of a superior manager— and the rewards can be substantial. For one thing, the manager is likely to have a higher proportion of strongly motivated people who do not need constant direction and control, which will leave her with more time to do the tasks she likes to do, to make improvements and plan for progress in her department, and to devise strategies for her own advancement. Furthermore, every employee who succeeds at a job, and possibly moves on to better opportunities in the organization, represents a success indicator for the manager who helped that employee.

The pleasure factor must also be considered. It cannot be much fun believing that the most important function you perform as a manager is keeping a group of employees on a performance norm. There is much more gratification in making it possible for a number of people to realize their talents and to apply them to your objectives with increasing proficiency. Employees can be a resource to you, in the attainment of both short-term and long-term objectives. Since they can and do talk with others in the organization about your outstanding skills as a manager, you benefit from some good publicity. People who are well treated are usually more committed to their work and more willing to share their innovative ideas with you. You will find that many of your employees want to make you look good in the organization; they identify with your pride and ambitions, and they have their own. They can also help you test out ideas and proposals before you try to sell them to higher management. That way, people to whom you report don't know about your bombs; they can see a greater proportion of probable successes thanks to the expertness and collaboration of your subordinates. When the necessity arises, employees will share some of your responsibilities and burdens. For example, during your prolonged absence, or during a temporary imbalance in the workload, the employees who work for you can set up their own assignment and coordination system that will permit uninterrupted operation for a time.

There are many opportunities for the people who work for you to enhance your success and advancement—especially if they are convinced that you want *them* to succeed and advance (which many managers do not) and that their own progress can be enhanced by yours.

SPECIAL PROBLEMS OF THE NEW MANAGER

The newly appointed woman manager often comes to her leadership position with less training and development than a male manager, and this lesser preparation can spell problems for her (although it is safe to say that much of the management education her male peers have received will prove to be less than useful). Frequently she is not taken seriously at first by many men (and women) in the organization. And some of these people will be watching and waiting for every misstep, hoping she will fail.

In organizations that have not previously provided opportunities for women above lower salary levels, the woman manager may feel quite lonely. There is no way for her to gain acceptance and blend in immediately as a new male manager does. She is a different quantity—and quality.

The woman manager will have to make her own way. But she should not ignore the organizational culture. This culture reflects the prevailing values of the company's management, and the reward system is based on these values. For example, an autocratic culture would reflect higher management's conviction that decision-making power must be concentrated in a few hands at the top, that the organization should be controlled, that employees should work according to regulations, and that information should be disseminated strictly on a need-to-know basis. Say you entered such a system and, because of your strong anti-autocratic values, tried to establish within your area of responsibility a counterculture in which employees participated in all major decisions affecting them and communication was open. You might find that you had created not only suspicion and disfavor at the top, but even anxiety among your employees. They would recognize that you were heading for a confrontation you were unlikely to win.

We are not advocating conformity, nor wholesale acceptance of a culture that is alien to your values. But you do have to be aware that a radical departure from what prevails can threaten the establishment and bring problems down on you.

As women move into more responsible positions, they are bound to encounter some men (and women) who are reluctant to work for them. There is nothing easy about having to listen while an employee says that what he has against you is the fact that you're female. You may be brilliant, an outstanding manager, a winner in every way. But he doesn't want to work with or for you.

Of course the reason he gives may be something else. But it will no doubt be clear to you what the problem is. One young marketing director who inherited her secretary from another department learned through the grapevine that the secretary was quite vague in telling others about where she now worked, and she was telling friends she thought she would get a new job elsewhere. The new manager had a long talk with the secretary, and the truth came out: the secretary felt she had received a demotion in status by being assigned to work for a woman.

There will be men who fear such a loss of status in the eyes of others. Some will feel a threat to their masculinity—the only women who have been in a superior position to them have been their mothers. Others will be apprehensive that they will not be able to throw off the conditioning that tells them men and women have primarily sexual relationships.

There is perhaps no way to deal with this problem head on. Awareness or consciousness-raising groups for men and women could help. But most organizations have done little experimentation in this area. So you're stuck with the task of having to win over subordinates who don't want to work for a woman.

In most cases in which you suspect sexism, you won't be very useful in trying to get the person to own up to it. Accept the reason he gives you for wanting to resign or transfer out; let him know, if he is worth keeping, that you regret losing him. Make it possible for him to talk with whomever he wishes. Give time a chance to work. Many such men have been able to work through their anxiety when their bosses took care not to reinforce it. Some new managers believe they have a right to demand full respect and loyalty from the outset. But most employees won't agree. Nor is it easy to understand how these managers would be content with such easily transferable or assignable loyalties or with respect that is given because it has been commanded.

We are hardly suggesting that you treat apprehensive people with tender, loving care. It might be the worst thing you could do. You have to go on being yourself, operating as you think best. It is really up to the employee to make the adjustment. It is *his* conditioning that is debilitating.

From time to time one hears a man or a woman say, "I've worked for a woman. But I'll never do it again." With all of the other challenges and opportunities facing you, you really don't need to put up with such recalcitrance (which, hopefully, will become rarer). Of course, there will be employees who won't like you—and their dislike may be based in part on the fact that you are a woman. But if they perform well under your guidance and direction, and are not offensive, their biases are their business.

You may also have to deal with the employee who sees you as a mother figure. You may not need a child, but you have one. An employee seeking this relationship will bring you all of his problems, including personal ones. He will work to build a special relationship with you. Should he come to work and find you not in your office, he'll be uneasy until he finds out why you aren't there. This type of dependent subordinate can turn on you, if he is feeling rebellious, because he is in some ways still an adolescent.

It is a relationship that you may wish to tolerate if the employee is highly valued. But you should be aware that it may annoy other employees or even arouse their resentment. This can be said of any relationship between boss and subordinate that is seen as privileged, or that seems to exclude others or put them at a disadvantage.

The above are some of the special considerations and problems that the woman manager needs to anticipate. A few, like organizational culture, may be beyond her influence. The rest of this chapter will be devoted to those factors that she can control: upgrading resources, achieving her goals, self-improvement, motivation, and others.

THE SUPERIOR MANAGER

Managers get characterized as authoritarian or autocratic, democratic, laissez-faire, and so on. These labels are sometimes useful to describe the prevailing attitude of the organization. But people are difficult to label. Even the most rigid person conforming to principle will from time to time and situation to situation exhibit unpredictable behavior.

One of the problems about talking in terms of managerial style is that a manager may believe she is acting in accordance with a particular style when, as far as the perceptions of employees are concerned, she is not.

Labels and categories are very seductive. Psychologist, professor, writer, and *manager* Douglas McGregor discovered this in the early 1960s when he published his now famous Theory X-Theory Y.[1] Theory X assumes that people really don't want to work, that they would do nothing in preference to working if they could get away with it, and that they must be coerced and controlled if they are to accomplish anything on the job. Theory Y, on the other hand, assumes that people really do like to work, that they have goals they want to achieve through that work, that most people seek responsibility (rather than avoid it), that most people are imaginative and creative, and that their intellects are underutilized.

To McGregor's distress, managers began to talk about Theory X-Theory Y as either-or, mutually exclusive, or as styles of management. McGregor was trying to describe two sets of assumptions on which people may base their perspectives of employees. He wasn't trying to formulate a management style—and he wasn't defining the worker.

One very important contribution made by Douglas McGregor was to alert people to the possibility that they might be approaching situations and people with invariable assumptions or preconceptions. Ironically, many who read or heard about Theory Y unquestioningly adopted its assumptions as the way to operate, which was not what McGregor had in mind. The point is that there are people who do not especially care about their jobs. For them it is a means of subsistence; they do not, through those jobs, achieve meaningful psychological, intellectual, spiritual, or artistic goals. Some people are not motivated to develop and demonstrate creativity on or off the job. Their work may have to be monitored, set for them, controlled, and checked. And the manager who bases her approach to these employees on Theory Y is going to be very frustrated indeed. Other people seem to want to be creative and enthusiastic but cannot find the key to involvement, to making the work meaningful. They may need a manager's help—or another job.

Obviously you have certain attitudes, biases, sets. You are in part a product of your conditioning. Thus, your dealings with people and situations will have a certain consistency about them. That fact reflects neither virtue nor vice—necessarily. What is essential is that you sometimes lessen the influence of your attitudes on your behavior—or disengage the two almost completely. For example, you may disdain any behavior that seems dictatorial. And yet there may be an occasion when you must adopt such behavior.

Situations—and people—differ. You may run a department in which employees are encouraged to develop their own means to accomplish their ends, in which people who are involved in and affected by decisions participate in making them, in which people are given opportunities to do trial-and-error experimentation. But suddenly you are faced with an emergency—an inescapable slash in the budget, a temporary work overload, a shorter than usual deadline. You decide to marshal your resources under your direct control. You unilaterally impose certain rules for the duration. You insist that all decisions and authorizations be cleared through you. In short, you act in an autocratic manner. You are aware of it, and you may very well be completely justified in doing so.

Unfortunately, there is often a gap between the way people believe they behave in a situation and the way others see their behavior. For that reason, a manager needs feedback from others. Without feedback, a manager can convince herself that she is acting in a certain manner, when in fact others see her behavior quite differently. We know of a woman manager who believes that she operates in a generally democratic, sharing manner. Yet her subordinates complain that she imposes her decisions on them and that she jealously guards her prerogatives as a manager. The startling discrepancy between how this manager behaves and how she thinks she behaves exists because she has long discouraged feedback from employees (most likely without knowing it).

This is a common problem. Every manager runs the risk of losing touch with her subordinates and their perceptions of how she operates. To avoid this, it is essential to encourage open communication and honesty between those who report to you.

Getting Feedback from Your Subordinates

Even when managers honestly seek subordinates' views on new projects, they often get no more than affirmative responses. For some people, the fact that it's the boss's plan turns a suggestion into a sacred cow. Subordinates may keep silent when they consider their boss's proposals second-rate or even potentially disastrous. They may tell themselves that they don't want to rock the boat or get into a hassle. Their real motive, however, is fear of offending the person who holds the key to their future.

Problems are bound to spring up when a less-than-good idea makes the grade simply because it's your brainchild. All too often, you are so close to your own ideas that you can't judge them objectively. For your own self-protection, you should seek the honest opinions of others.

There are some things you can do to be sure you're getting honest opinions. First, you have to be clear on your motives. Do you truly want the other person to level with you? Are you prepared to listen to adverse comments without becoming defensive or tuning them out? If you say "Would you help me on this? I'd like to get any suggestions you may have" or "This is a bit rough. I have a feeling I haven't touched all the bases," the employee then won't get the feeling he has to come out with a flat verdict of good or bad.

Keep in mind that people are generally hesitant about making changes in what seems like the final version of a plan. Therefore, it's a good idea to let subordinates see it before the final typing stage. Consider providing them with copies typed with extra wide margins and encouraging them to jot down their comments.

If you don't provide each of your subordinates with a copy of the plan, you should still get the opinions of at least two of them. When a subordinate knows he isn't the only one who has been asked for his views, there is a greater likelihood of his leveling, because he doesn't bear the whole burden.

In most instances, it takes more than a "What do you think?" to get the full story. To accept the other person's opinion without probing to find the basis for it and asking for elaboration cuts off a promising source of ideas.

Your tone of voice and facial expression can be all-important here. If you appear at all defensive or impatient, you won't get any further useful response. A deep frown or an overaggressive reaction, such as "I don't understand your suggestion; what is it you're driving at?" can shut off the flow of words as effectively as an open threat.

Even if you have already anticipated the faults or defects that a subordinate brings up in discussing a plan, it's a good idea to explore them once again with the employee. The amount of honest feedback you get in the future depends on your patience and receptivity now.

Developing Mutual Understanding

One of the most effective ways to help, understand, and sympathize with your subordinates is to allow them to relate to you in the same way. Giving and getting are naturally complementary roles in human relationships. The boss-employee relationship is at its best, therefore, when both parties share in the giving *and* the receiving.

Here are some considerations to help you evaluate your own attitude toward making mutual understanding and assistance a two-way street:

Do you believe that the people who report to you have talents outside their specific job responsibilities? Unless you do, you cannot expect them to respond to your problems or your needs.

Do you believe that admitting problems to, or receiving help from, subordinates diminishes you as a manager? If you do, you will not be able to let employees know what's on your mind, thereby assuring that they will never be able to help. While people respect a manager for her competence, they still see her as a human being. And every human being has problems, and can use help in solving them. By openly admitting that you, too, have needs, you will gain more respect than if you try to hide behind an impossible-to-believe shield of imperturbability.

Do you believe that people who have different perspectives from yours may still be able to offer solutions to your problems? Your subordinates may not view your problems the way you do—but that doesn't preclude the possibility that they'll be helpful.

Do you believe that people like to help and like to feel they've accomplished something important? Being able to help someone else is personally gratifying. Why deny employees—and yourself— these mutual benefits?

Of course, in setting up a climate of mutual understanding and assistance, you must also determine your needs and how the people who report to you can help you to fulfill them. Obviously, your primary need is to carry out your own work goals and objectives. Yet employees seldom understand exactly what their boss's goals are. Once they understand what you're aiming for, however, they can start thinking of their own work in those terms.

Another need may be to solve specific problems in fulfilling these goals and objectives. Do you tell the people in your department about the problems you are facing? Too often, employees only find out what troubles their manager has when she tells them how she intends to solve the problem. When you clue people in to difficult situations, you give them a chance to suggest possible ways of eliminating the problems.

Most managers also need feedback and reassurance. It's good to know what people think, how they react to something you have done. But does it ever occur to you to ask them for their opinion? Sometimes the direct approach is the most effective: ask and you greatly increase your chances of being answered.

Considering Your Employees' Personal Goals

In almost any survey of managers and their problems, the responses will show that "motivation of employees" is a number one or two priority. Many managers, even though they may be intellectually convinced that *they* do not motivate others (that people motivate themselves), undoubtedly keep hoping that they'll find the formula for getting employees to behave the way they want them to behave.

One of the best explanations of motivation in people at work has been offered by Victor Vroom, now a professor at Yale.[2] Putting his model simply, a person's motivation is determined by how much he or she values the task and whether he or she feels capable of doing it.

To illustrate, suppose you offer a key assistant her choice of two positions. She is bright, helpful, dedicated, and ambitious. The first job is a newly created responsibility. It is not quite clear what skills will be needed, but the rewards for doing the job well will be substantial. The second job is a traditional one. It represents no essential break from the kind of work she is doing now; the advancement will be minor; and there will be no distinguished opportunities later.

To your surprise and disappointment, your ambitious subordinate chooses the safer job. What happened was that while she found the prospect of doing the first job more valuable, she also felt the chances of succeeding at it were low. She may have feared that she lacked the skills, or that she would not be given everything she required to do the job as it needed to be done. Whether the difficulty was internal or external, and despite the value she placed on the opportunity, she doubted her chances of success. The other job offered less value but a high probability of success. Value times probability produces force. And people tend to make decisions and to act on the highest positive force—or, in some cases, on the least negative force. They will choose the option that has the most value to them and the highest probability of success. Or, faced with unpleasant alternatives, they tend to select the least distasteful one.

Although greatly simplified here, the Vroom expectancy model is still useful for explaining a person's behavior in certain situations. The model further suggests that a manager must consider the value an employee places on a task or job together with the employee's expectancy of succeeding at it in order to properly manage that employee's work. Obviously, when the manager must concern herself with the values, goals, and expectancies of every employee, her job becomes tremendously complex. Perhaps that is one reason why so many managers think in terms of groups of people and settle for getting adequate performance from the group as a whole.

Highly motivated people are usually goal-oriented. But their goals are defined differently. Some people do indeed work primarily for the money. Others like the money but derive the greatest satisfaction or reward from knowing they have performed in an outstanding and skillful manner. There are almost infinite varieties of goals—or rewards that people seek through work: power, advancement, freedom, esteem, fame, professional expertise. A manager need not know the personal goals of the people who work for her to convey her interest in having them realized.

However, a manager will often broadcast the message that she is not really involved with the employee's goals. Management by objectives (MBO) programs, in which everyone is supposed to participate in setting goals, have foundered because management saw only the importance of organizational goals. For some reason the belief has persisted that organizational goals become relevant to employees if you break them down into sufficiently small units so that the employees can see how what they do will contribute to the whole. But if you are to be effective in persuading employees to be committed to the goals you want to achieve, you must find ways to ask them what they want to get out of all this.

A follow-up question is, "What do you want out of your job?" Referring back to the Vroom model, employees are more likely to invest their energies in tasks or goals that seem valuable to them and in which they feel the probability of success is sufficiently high. If the employees' goals are meaningful to you (will contribute to the realization of organizational goals), it behooves you as manager to help increase the probability of their achieving them.

It takes time and effort on your part to build trust to a level where employees will tell you about their goals and how they fit in with the overall efforts to achieve organizational goals. Too many managers try to achieve this openness in annual or semi-annual interviews, usually in connection with a formal appraisal or goal-setting program. But such formal sessions should be supplemented by periodic informal conversations.

The Manager as Coach

"Coaching" refers to discussions between a manager and subordinate that contribute to the latter's improvement and higher effectiveness. It is probably one of the most important activities of a manager in upgrading his resources—yet it is often neglected.

In many cases, the reason for this neglect is one that an executive would prefer not to face. That phrase "growth and development" sounds great when it is applied to the executive. But to her subordinates? Why should she help them grow out of her department? Why should she develop someone who may then get ambitions to take over her job?

The fact is that a manager who ignores her coaching responsibilities limits her own job and pays a penalty for doing so. Whatever her actual title, she reduces her role, so far as subordinates are concerned, to that of mere supervision. She rejects a chance to initiate change in favor of merely reacting to it when and if it occurs. Most important, she deprives herself of the talents and capabilities of her employees that could contribute to her own success as leader of a team and enhance her own managerial reputation.

The manager who accepts her coaching responsibilities, and sees the possible advantages to herself inherent in them, may nonetheless have some problems in working out a course of action. Even in organizations that have formal periodic performance appraisals that involve some coaching, she may not get much benefit from those occasional interviews. Frequently, the framework for the interview is prescribed by top management, with all the emphasis on getting the information needed to fill in a narrowly focused evaluation form. Questions that aren't on the form just don't get asked. Moreover, the amount of time allotted for the interviews may be too short for the manager to update her knowledge of what the employees really need in order to grow in their jobs. As mentioned earlier, such formal interviews need to be supplemented with informal ones.

Informal talks with each subordinate are only a preliminary, however, to the formulation of a growth and development program that brings results. For that, a systematic approach is necessary with equal emphasis on three points:

1. Set up your own "data bank." Take notes immediately after your conversation with each subordinate. Otherwise you will probably forget some of the areas you've covered. Also, if something was said or hinted at that alerted you to a quality you never knew the person had, adding it immediately to your notes will give you still more to build on. And make a note to yourself to follow up each interview at a specific time in the future, to ensure the continuation of the program.

2. Present specific guidelines. "Growth and development" is in itself an amorphous phrase, which may be another reason managers have difficulty in coming to grips with it. Giving shape to a growth and development program is a task that requires managerial imagination—and precision. Subsequent discussions with the subordinate should point to specific developmental experiences, such as further training or education, a field trip, servicing a key account,

temporary duty in another department, a new assignment. And these suggestions, too, should be added to your notes.

Aside from the benefits to the employees, working within this framework gives you a reason to keep in touch with them. And this is important, not only because it will keep the growth and development program alive (and structured), but because it makes your concern, as well as your expectations, convincing to subordinates.

3. Touch all bases. A good growth and development plan should include everyone in the department. (Keeping a record for each employee is a way of making sure there is full coverage.) This is not just a matter of fairness, though that can be useful in maintaining morale. It is also a way to avoid the pitfall of depending on "indispensable" people who may fall ill, take early retirement, or quit. There may be other "indispensables" in your department that you will discover through your talks with them.

The validity of a development plan rests on how it suits each individual—and that requires checking back. What struck you as an ideal developmental experience may have left the employee cold. You may need to offer another suggestion or to probe more closely into the employee's aspirations and capabilities as he or she sees them.

It's wise to keep in mind that people change, even though outwardly they may seem the same. Thus, an employee who states that she has "no interest" in going into management may later regret her flat negative—and not know how to retract it unless given an opportunity to do so. Or she may have been talking without knowing what management opportunities were available or what they involved.

Conducting informal interviews in a way that the manager knows is regular but that seems casual to employees—and hence not tension-producing—offers her a chance to bring her own perceptions of the people in her department up to date. And she can use these occasions to help them broaden their own thinking as well.

Reinforcing the Behavior You Want

As manager, one of your most important jobs is to help employees develop more effective behavior in order to reach the objectives you have agreed upon. Positive reinforcement is a technique that many managers have found useful in encouraging employees to develop more effective ways of acting. The essence of positive reinforcement is that you reward the behavior you want, and you don't reward the behavior you don't want.

A simple example: your secretary is careless about typing your letters. You want her to be more careful. The steps you have taken so far are anything but clear-cut. Occasionally you've gotten angry when the mistake was serious. On a couple of occasions, when the typo was funny, you joked about it. Other times you didn't say a word; you simply signed the letter.

If you want to encourage your secretary to change, follow these steps:

Define what you want. You want letters with *no* mistakes.

Don't make a big deal about a mistake. Simply point it out and hand back the letter for retyping.

Give recognition for a good job. Don't be extravagant in your praise; that can be regarded as insulting. Something like "You did a good job; I really appreciate how well that looks" is usually enough.

In the beginning, give positive feedback and recognition often. You don't have to give a compliment every time, but in the beginning it is best to give praise often. Later, as your secretary becomes more proficient, and mistakes are infrequent, you might want to give compliments on an occasional basis.

Give feedback immediately. Be sure to call attention to the desired behavior as soon as you see it, if possible. Too much time between the act and the praise dulls the impact of the reinforcement.

Be specific about feedback. "You're doing a nice job; keep it up" is usually not as effective in encouraging an employee to continue to do what you want as is something like, "You deserve a medal for getting all those letters out so fast without mistakes. That was great work."

Be consistent. Most people have the best intentions of reinforcing desired behavior, but then they get busy or for some other reason neglect the reinforcement schedule. That schedule—consistent recognition of desired behavior—is absolutely vital while the employee is still struggling to change.

Don't emphasize the negative side. The employee will be discouraged if you give the impression that the wrong work occurs much more frequently than the right work. Also, if you make too much of a fuss over mistakes, you can't be sure of what you are reinforcing.

Don't be manipulative. Be open about the behavior you want and what you are doing to encourage it.

Positive reinforcement is a reward for doing the right thing. The reward may be praise or public recognition. In certain situations you may pay more money in wages and salary, or give a bonus, a promotion, or greater responsibilities—all of these can be legitimate and effective reinforcements.

Upgrading Your Resources

The woman who has had to work hard (in most cases much harder than a man) to be admitted to what was formerly an all-male enclave and has had to demonstrate time and time again her superior qualifications and intense drive is sometimes shocked to find that inside the management preserve the criteria that were applied to judge her worthiness on the way up are definitely not continually applied to those who have gained admission. While this may not be true of all organizations, it can be said generally that the hard-driving, innovative, growth-oriented manager who is forever pushing up the standard is not the rule. No matter how much these characteristics are publicized as prerequisites for advancement into managerial ranks, they are usually not required for continuing membership.

If you are in a typical organization, you could not be blamed for suspecting that the reward system encourages mediocrity, not superiority. You may find that what are admired most are the abilities to adjust to the norms and values of the informal group—the managerial club—to conform (or, less harshly, to accept the constraints on rocking the boat), and to compete with peers without being embarrassingly aggressive. The glib counsel, "To get along, go along," if followed, will increase a manager's value as a member of the team.

The conditions that we have described above pose a potential conflict for many men and women. We are not saying that superior performance will not be rewarded or that there is no way to the executive suite for the exceptional person, although many would have you believe that this is the case. The one-dimensional view of progress says that if you want to get ahead, you have to please your superiors. According to the two-dimensional view, you have to please your superiors but you also have to be known as a person who can get along with her peers. The three-dimensional view is that, in addition to being an asset to higher management and your peers, you must also do a good job for the employees who work for you. If you do all this, it's unlikely that you'll stay where you are. You'll be pushed upward.

What does it mean to do a good job for your employees? It means continually upgrading employees as resources—to you, to themselves, and to the organization—helping them grow, giving them opportunities to develop their skills (and insisting that they do so), and increasing their responsibilities. It also means replacing those whose performance, commitment, and growth lag behind the others and your notion of what is minimally acceptable.

If you did nothing else, the continuing efforts to upgrade the quality of your operation would stamp you as unusual. Many managers start out with the objective of building a superior work group, but they stop when they reach a level of quality that is acceptable to the organization.

Why? It's a drain on the budget. It costs money to recruit people (although eventually the cost is more than repaid in the better performance). It's risky. The present employees are known quantities; replacements, no matter how impressive their records and credentials, have to prove themselves on your payroll. It's tough emotionally. Firing employees is no fun. Replacements need training, and training takes away time from other tasks. But many managers have training skills beneath their noses that they are not utilizing: certain employees will find an occasional training assignment challenging and exciting. A continual upgrading that means higher and higher standards and the elimination of people who cannot keep up need not adversely affect morale. But it could if a manager's measurements of performance are arbitrary, if goals are not clearly established for all to understand, and if employees cannot relate to those goals.

Here is a partial list of the components of a successful upgrading program:

—A clear definition of goals to be achieved and/or standards to be met.
—Understanding and acceptance of those goals and standards by employees (who, hopefully, have participated in establishing them).
—Measurement of progress or performance (through a timetable, subgoals, level of productivity averaged over a realistic period, and so on).
—Feedback to employees.
—Probation for employees who show less than acceptable performance. Reward for those who meet or exceed goals and standards.
—Termination of employees who have been unsuccessful in the probationary period.

Sticking to clear performance measurements and timetables is essential to the success of your upgrading effort. Otherwise employees may feel you are discriminatory or arbitrary (you bend for this person but not for that one). You should not rule out the occasional exception because of conditions beyond the employee's control or temporarily distracting personal problems. Another reason for sticking to measurements and timetables is that they help you avoid investing a disproportionate amount of time and energy in trying to improve the performance of less productive employees (a mistake made by so many managers). Most of your time and energy should be directed to aiding those who may not seem to require your help. Let's use a sales analogy as an illustration. If as a sales manager your aim was to help your salespeople increase their effectiveness in selling, where would you place your priority? On *A,* who produces $200,000 in volume, or on *B,* who brings in

$100,000? Many managers would consider *B* a priority. There is, they might say, so much room for improvement (and so much glory for the manager who makes a good producer out of one who is average). The fallacy that many managers fall prey to is in thinking that the amount of time spent to increase *A*'s results by, say, 5 percent could help raise *B*'s production by 15 to 20 percent. Generally, however, managers will find that even to help *B* make the same percentage gain as *A* will take more time.

Things seldom work out as cleanly as in our brief example, but you will be surprised by the overall results of providing special assistance, training and development, and coaching and guidance to those who are already doing very well—because these employees will be building on a broader and deeper base of strengths and skills. Furthermore, at least some of them will regard your special efforts as recognition and reward for their outstanding performance. Hence, accomplishing the goals you and they have agreed on will have an even greater value (and your help will increase their expectancy of success).

We have saved the most unpleasant aspect of upgrading your work force for last. Few managers relish the idea of firing employees. In fact, some so loathe the task that they will keep incompetent employees long after their incompetence has become plain to everyone. Such delays are expensive, morale-eroding, and demotivating to others. Other managers try to place incompetent employees in "harmless" jobs—ones that don't carry enough authority and autonomy to cause much damage. (That may be understandable in the case of an employee who has been with the organization for many years but who is a year or two too young to retire.)

Thus the marginal performers hang around, creating problems for the managers, for themselves, for co-workers—and even for outsiders who have to deal with them. The employees won't take the initiative to get out and seek jobs for which they are better qualified. The managers will have to do that for them.

Reducing the Pain in Firing Someone

Firing an employee is never easy, even when the reasons are clear and the individual has received ample warning. Nevertheless, when the deed has to be done, some ways of doing it are better than others because they're more thoughtful and humane—and thus, in the end, more helpful to both the manager who faces the unpleasant task of letting someone go and the person who is being terminated.

In your attempt to be humane, there are certain traps you should avoid. First, don't use the "no-fault" approach. "It's just not working out" may be the true reason for termination in some cases—as when the job is being phased out or the company is reversing a bad decision—but in most cases the statement is a means of self-protection. The firer does not even say "You're not working out" or "I made a mistake," because she does not want to get into a discussion of where the employee—or she—failed. All the stunned ex-employee knows is that the rug has been pulled out from under him.

The "you'll be better off" approach may also reflect the truth—sometimes a job doesn't measure up to a person's talents—but in other cases, the manager who says "I think you're suited to something more creative than this job provides" often is trying to avoid criticism of herself or the other person.

Again, the fired subordinate isn't being told anything helpful, since, in most cases, he was willing to do the kind of job for which he was hired. Nothing is said about why he was put in the job to begin with or in what ways he failed to meet his employer's expectations. And if the employee leaves with the feeling that it wasn't his fault (when it really was), he'll learn nothing that will help him in his next job.

There are times when good people have to be fired for no other reason than that the company can no longer afford their services, even if they have been excellent. In these situations the "I cry for you" approach may seem to be the best one. But some managers tend to sympathize to excess: "You know how much we've always thought of you here. It breaks my heart to let you go, but we have to because of the damned budget."

A better technique involves calling the employee into your office and saying, simply, "There isn't any easy way to do this. I have to let you go." You then stop and give the other person time to get over the shock. Then if the employee protests or wants further explanation—as is usually the case—you can say, "I'll talk with you about it if you like, but you must understand that I have no other alternative. Perhaps if we discussed it, we'd both learn something that would help us in the future.''

There are also certain positive steps that can reduce the pain of dismissal for both parties.

Get to the point. If you are about to fire a person, don't make small talk first. This is an extremely tense moment, and trying to make it casual will increase the tension. If you focus on the person, together with the circumstances that have brought about the dismissal, you'll probably find yourself speaking honestly and helpfully.

Use only firsthand data to justify the firing. Let's suppose the reason for dismissal is inadequate performance. You have also heard that the person has had a lot of personality problems with other people in the department—though never with you. Since these are not the reasons for dismissal, mentioning them, even though they may have affected the employee's work, is unlikely to serve a useful purpose. It will make the employee even more defensive than he is already.

Try to minimize the blow to the person's ego. The moment of firing is not the time to make suggestions about how the individual can improve his character, learning ability, and so on. The object is to dismiss the person, not destroy him. Someone who is being fired deserves to be protected from feelings of self-doubt, defeat, and depression. And though the truth should be told, it should be cast in a form that will allow the fired person to think positively about himself.

Be helpful. If you can help the person find another job, there is every reason to do so. For example, offer to write a letter or make a phone call to a prospective employer; suggest other companies to approach; give information and reassurance about severance pay, continuation of health insurance, use of the office, and so forth.

When you fire employees, you should consider the attitude that the fired persons are going to take along when they leave. If they leave with the impression that you did only what you had to do, that you were fair, objective, and as supportive as possible, the subordinates are not likely to carry a grudge against you or the company. After all, there's always a chance that you'll have to deal with someone you've fired again someday—perhaps as a customer or a supplier. The other thing to consider is how you're going to feel about yourself after the persons leave. If you know you've done your level best to sustain their self-respect, you've gone a long way toward sustaining your own.

THE ESSENCE OF SUCCESSFUL MANAGEMENT

An effective manager never stops learning. There will always be some situations in which you will be less effective than you want to be and in which you can improve. In every work environment there are variables such as organizational culture and values, priorities demanded by higher management, constraints and requirements imposed by outside contacts, and frequently changing relationships with bosses, peers, and subordinates. All of these dynamics can be altered by crises; change of people, structure, or size; new customers, markets, objectives, or technology. The list is virtually endless. The manager must learn to deal with each new dynamic. Principles of management are taught in classrooms, defined in books, expounded by veteran managers. But the skills lie in knowing how and when to apply those principles. Because of the innumerable variables, a manager will find it difficult to determine how to apply her skills until the problem, opportunity, or challenge is clear enough to be defined.

Effective management, therefore, is a continuing process of diagnosis, analysis, formulation and re-formulation as situations arise. The unceasing need to learn, expand, and shape new behavior is too much for many managers—and for many people who are not managers. They reach plateaus. They rely increasingly on old formulas for dealing with new and different situations. They drift, lose control, become obsolescent. It is an unusual organization that does not have its community of managers, professionals, and other employees who, with the passage of time, talk more about past accomplishments, venerate traditional ways of doing things, and restrict the freedom of others to initiate change. To this community, principles and policies become inordinately important.

But the manager must deal with people who, unlike principles and policies, change—perhaps only in small ways—daily. They become more competent—or less. They respond to problems and challenges more effectively—or less. They interact with each other more constructively—or less.

These statements are true of people in general. The successful manager is really the successful *person*. You have goals that are meaningful to you, and you assume that others have goals important to them also, even if you don't always know what they are.

You don't like to be treated as everyone else is treated, because you know that no other person in the world has precisely the same knowledge, talent, conditioning, and upbringing as you. You assume therefore that others see themselves as somewhat unique and don't wish to be lumped together with everyone else.

You need psychological space to move around in, to be able to select options. You don't like to be hemmed in, deprived of freedom. You imagine that others appreciate having space too.

You want to be liked—but even more, you want to be respected. And you don't question the notion that others want to be respected also.

You know that you are a biased person. There are bound to be gaps between what you think you do or say and how others perceive you. You realize that the only chance you have of becoming a more complete person is to get feedback and encouragement from others. And you know how much others must depend on you for the same feedback and encouragement.

You know it's healthy and growth-producing for you to be able to work through problems and conflicts with others and obstacles they put in your path, often unwittingly. There is no reason for you to believe that others don't wish to be able to work through difficulties with you.

To your distress, you sometimes act from less than honorable motivations. But you see yourself as essentially honest, a person of good will, trying to get along with others and not to hurt them. You know it is helpful to remind yourself that most others see themselves the same way.

In one form or another, you've heard the above truths expressed throughout your life, often in easy-to-take aphorisms. They seem simplistic, perhaps even corny sometimes. And since managing has become a sophisticated science—and an art—it may seem rather primitive to discuss what seem to be complex interpersonal relationships in such elementary, rather old-hat terms.

Each situation you encounter as a manager will be somewhat different from every other situation, will require its own diagnosis, analysis, and application of this technique or that. But your growth as a manager—even more important, as a person—will be considerably enhanced if you consistently grant other persons the same virtues you perceive in yourself, and allow them the same deficiencies that in your more introspective moments you admit in yourself. The accuracy of your judgments will vary from person to person—and in some cases you will be too condemning or too generous. But in most situations, giving others the same benefits you give yourself will provide you with a substantial head start in achieving helpful, progressive, constructive relationships that will enhance your professional and personal growth.

REFERENCES

1. Douglas McGregor, *The Human Side of Enterprise* (New York: McGraw-Hill, 1960), pp. 33–34.
2. Victor H. Vroom, *Work and Motivation* (New York: Wiley, 1964).

RESOURCE LIST

Employment Agencies, Search Firms, and Job-Hunting Services

ALUMNAE ADVISORY CENTER, INC., 541 Madison Ave., New York, N.Y. 10022.

Nonprofit organization that helps college women of all ages plan their careers. Supported by 38 women's and coeducational colleges and universities. Reductions in placement fees are available to alumnae of these colleges and universities and to women who become associate members of the AAC (annual cost: $35). AAC also publishes booklets on writing application letters, preparing résumés, job interviews, and other job-related topics, as well as Job Fact Sheets on over 50 occupations such as law, merchandising, and purchasing.

CALIFORNIA AFFIRMATIVE ACTION, 180 Harbor Drive, Sausalito, Calif. 94965.

Communication organization that places women, minorities, and others in all types of jobs at no charge. (Firm is underwritten by employer-members.)

CATALYST, 6 East 82nd St., New York, N.Y. 10028.

Founded in 1962 by five college presidents to help women prepare for and obtain top business and professional jobs, and to create more job opportunities for women. The organization provides vocational and educational guidance, information on workshops and programs, and assistance in job hunting. Women seeking counseling and placement fill out precoded questionnaires which are processed by computer to produce profiles that are made available to Catalyst affiliates, employers, and educators. Catalyst also sells booklets such as "Your Job Campaign" and "How to Hunt for a Job" and a Career Opportunity Series of reports on over 60 occupations (accounting, data processing, personnel, etc.).

DISTAFFERS INCORPORATED, 1315 Walnut Street, Suite 918, Philadelphia, Pa. 19107.

A service that specializes in the placement of professional women in full- or part-time positions.

LEAR, PURVIS, WALKER & CO., 1901 Ave. of the Stars, Los Angeles, Calif. 90067.

Search firm that specializes in placement of women and minorities in jobs $10,000 and up.

MANAGEMENT WOMAN, INC., The Plaza at 59th St., New York N.Y. 10019.
Executive recruitment and search firm that specializes in positions for middle- and upper-level management women.

MILLER GREENE ASSOCIATES, INC., Division of Brentwood Personnel Associates, Inc., 1280 Rt. 46, Parsippany, N.J. 07054.
Employment agency that specializes in financial, marketing, and personnel jobs. Affiliated with National Personnel Associates, Inc., a network of more than 150 individually owned agencies in 50 cities that interexchanges résumés through a central distribution system. Especially useful for women who want to relocate. (To find an NPA-affiliated agency, look up NPA under ''Employment Agencies'' in the Yellow Pages.)

OPTIONS FOR WOMEN, 8419 Germantown Ave., Philadelphia, Pa. 19118.
A nonprofit, licensed employment agency, founded in 1970, which places women in a variety of full- and part-time positions—professional, managerial, and specialized—in the Philadelphia area. Also provides counseling and testing services.

SELECTIVITY INC., 7 Cypress Road, Lake Forrest Park, Natick, Mass. 01760.
A placement service and resource organization for educational and professional women. Owned and staffed by feminists fully experienced in business techniques.

THE TALENT BANK, National Federation of Business and Professional Women's Clubs, 2012 Massachusetts Ave. N.W., Washington, D.C. 20036.
Established in 1970, the Bank now contains data on several thousand women qualified to fill management positions in industry, government, and universities. The Federation serves as a clearinghouse in which 26 other women's organizations participate. To apply for inclusion, request a questionnaire form from NFBPW. (There is no charge to employer or job applicant.)

TODAY'S WOMAN, 21 Charles St., Westport, Conn. 06880.
A placement service that publishes a monthly list of job applicants which it sends to companies throughout the United States. Most of the candidates screened for positions are in the $10,000–30,000 salary range.

WOMEN'S CAREER CAUCUS, 645 No. Michigan Ave., Chicago, Ill. 60611.

Recruiting service firm that runs career conferences in which eligible candidates are interviewed by major companies.

WOMEN'S EDUCATIONAL & INDUSTRIAL UNION, Career Services Dept., 264 Boylston St., Boston, Mass. 02116.

One of the oldest nonprofit women's services in the U.S. Places women in business and professional jobs, full- and part-time, and provides free career counseling and other services.

WOMEN'S, INC., 15 Spinning Wheel. Rd. (Suite 14), Hinsdale, Ill. 60521.

Consulting firm with search division that recruits women for technical, sales, and management jobs (no fee). Another division provides counseling, testing, and career planning (for fee).

A directory of employment agencies, giving the employment specialties of each agency, is available from National Employment Association, 2000 K St. N.W., Washington, D.C. 20006 (Price: $3.60). Ask for the current issue of *Employment Directions*.

Professional Women's Groups

The groups listed below have channels through which women members may be referred for jobs, or they print listings of job openings in their newsletters. The groups marked by asterisk (*) have rosters of women members seeking jobs; these lists are available to prospective employers.

American Chemical Society, 1155 16th St. N.W., Washington, D.C. 20036

American Economic Association, 1313 21st Ave. South, Nashville, Tenn. 37207

American Mathematical Society, P.O. Box 6248, Providence, R.I. 02904

American Personnel and Guidance Association, 1607 New Hampshire Ave. N.W., Washington, D.C. 20009

American Physical Society, 335 E. 45th St., New York, N.Y. 10017 *

American Psychological Association, 1200 17th St. N.W., Washington, D.C. 20036

American Society of Biological Chemists, 9650 Rockville Pike, Bethesda, Md. 20014

American Society of Training and Development, 6414 Odana Rd., Madison, Wis. 53705

Association of American Law Schools, One Dupont Circle N.W., Washington, D.C. 20036 *

Association of Women in Architecture, P.O. Box 1, Clayton, Mo. 63105 *

Association for Women in Psychology, 7012 Western Ave., Chevy Chase, Md. 20015 *

Association of Women in Science, 1818 R St. N.W., Washington, D.C. 20009 *

National Association of Bank Women, 111 E. Wacker Drive, Chicago, Ill. 60601 *

Society of Women Engineers, 345 E. 47th St., New York, N.Y. 10017 *

More information about groups that promote career opportunities for professional women may be obtained from: Federation of Organizations for Professional Women, 1346 Connecticut Ave. N.W., Suite 1122, Washington, D.C. 20036. Additional information about women's groups that assist women seeking jobs is available from: Project on the Status and Education of Women, Association of American Colleges, 1818 R St. N.W., Washington, D.C. 20009.

Women's Business, Governmental, and Political Groups

AMERICAN BUSINESS WOMEN'S ASSOCIATION, 9100 Ward Parkway, Kansas City, Mo. 64114.

Founded in 1949, the ABWA has 1,200 local chapters that hold monthly meetings at which members hear business speakers and participate in activities. ABWA provides some scholarships and job-hunting assistance, as well as travel and insurance benefits, and publishes a magazine called *Women in Business*. Subscription price is $7 for nine issues a year; membership dues are $12 a year.

EQUAL EMPLOYMENT OPPORTUNITY COMMISSION, 1800 G St. N.W., Washington, D.C. 20506.

This agency was established by Title VII of the Civil Rights Act of 1964 as amended by the Equal Employment Opportunity Act of 1972. It enforces regulations to end discrimination based on race, color, religion, national origin, and, of course, sex—in hiring, promotion, firing, wages, testing, training, apprenticeship, and other conditions of employment. EEOC handles complaints about discrimination, issues publications, and provides other types of assistance for both employees and employers. It has regional offices in Boston, New York, Philadelphia, Atlanta, Chicago, Dallas, Kansas City, Mo., Denver, San Francisco, and Seattle, as well as a number of district offices. Information can be obtained from the Office of Public Affairs at the above address.

NATIONAL FEDERATION OF BUSINESS AND PROFESSIONAL WOMEN'S CLUBS, 2012 Massachusetts Ave. N.W., Washington, D.C. 20036.

This is one of the largest and oldest women's organizations, having been founded in 1919. It has about 4,000 local groups and over 50 state groups, plus a foundation that provides Career Advancement Scholarships. The Federation conducts management seminars and other programs, for which it charges nominal fees (about $30 for a two-day meeting, for example). Its magazine, *National Business Woman,* published eleven times a year, costs $5. Annual membership dues are approximately $6.

THE NATIONAL ORGANIZATION FOR WOMEN (NOW), 1957 East 73rd St. Chicago, Ill. 60649.

Established in 1966, this is the largest women's rights group in the United States. By mid-1974, it had 700 chapters and a membership of more than 36,000 (91 percent women). Also has a legal-defense and education fund.

WOMEN'S BUREAU, U.S. Department of Labor, 14th Street and Constitution Ave., Washington, D.C. 20210.

Central source of information within the federal government on matters relating to the economic, legal, and civil status of women; also develops policies and programs to promote better utilization of womanpower. Provides consultative and advisory services and technical assistance for employers, as well as information and publications for women. The Bureau has regional offices in Boston, New York, Philadelphia, Atlanta, Chicago, Dallas, Kansas City, Mo., Denver, San Francisco, and Seattle.

WOMEN'S EQUITY ACTION LEAGUE (WEAL), 538 National Press Bldg., Washington, D.C. 20004.

Organization established to improve the status of women through legislation, litigation, and education. Publishes a newsletter (*Washington Report*) and some other materials, such as a booklet titled "Suggestions for Preparing Résumés."

Women's Periodicals

The Executive Woman, 747 Third Ave., New York, N.Y. 10017.
Newsletter that features recent appointments and promotions of women (including "firsts"), special events, and meetings being held. Also includes a lead story on an eminent woman, a feature story on an informative subject such as writing a résumé or pension planning, and some classified advertisements. (6 pp., $20 a year for 10 issues)

The Spokeswoman, 5464 South Shore Drive, Chicago, Ill. 60515.
A monthly newsletter that covers major meetings, political and legal developments concerning women, and recently published books (written by women). Also includes several pages of Help Wanted ads, most of which are placed by companies, universities, and other large organizations. (10–12 pp., $7 a year for 12 issues)

Womanpower: "A Monthly Report on Fair Employment Practices for Women," Betsy Hogan Associates, 222 Rawson Road, Brookline, Mass. 02146.
Newsletter covering recent laws and regulations regarding women, and current trends. Usually has a number of items on complaints, lawsuits, court cases, and settlements, plus information on conferences, services, and publications available. (8 pp., $37 a year for 12 issues)

Women Today, Today Publications, 621 National Press Bldg., Washington, D.C. 20004.
Biweekly newsletter that covers major political, legislative, and educational developments. Also lists activities, meetings, projects, and programs of women's groups. Very government-oriented. (6 pp., $18 a year for 26 issues)

SELECTED READING

Bird, Caroline. *Everything a Woman Needs to Know to Get Paid What She's Worth*. New York: David McKay & Co., 1973.

Bird, Caroline, with Sara Wells Briller. *Born Female: The High Cost of Keeping Women Down*. Rev. ed. New York: David McKay & Co., 1970.

Crystal, John C., and Richard N. Bolles. *Where Do I Go from Here with My Life?* New York: The Seabury Press, 1974.

Drucker, Peter F., *Management: Tasks, Responsibilities, Practices*. New York: Harper & Row, 1974.

Epstein, Cynthia Fuchs. *Woman's Place*. Berkeley: University of California Press, 1971.

Ginzberg, Eli, and Alice M. Yohalem (eds). *Corporate Lib*. Baltimore: Johns Hopkins Press, 1973.

Huber, Joan (ed). *Changing Women in a Changing Society*. Chicago: University of Chicago Press, 1973.

James, Muriel, and Dorothy Jongeward. *Born to Win*. Reading, Mass.: Addison-Wesley, 1973.

Janeway, Elizabeth. *Between Myth and Morning*. New York: William Morrow & Co., 1974.

Jongeward, Dorothy, and Dru Scott. *Affirmative Action for Women: A Practical Guide*. Reading, Mass.: Addison-Wesley, 1973.

Schwartz, Felice N., Margaret H. Schifter, and Susan S. Gillotti. *How to Go to Work When Your Husband Is Against It, Your Children Aren't Old Enough, and There's Nothing You Can Do Anyhow*. New York: Simon & Schuster, 1972.

Taft, Renee. *Career Planning for College Women*. Washington, D.C.: Distaffers Research and Counseling Center, 1974.

Women's Bureau, Employment Standards Administration, U.S. Department of Labor. *Careers for Women in the 70s*. Washington, D.C.: 1973.

————. *A Working Woman's Guide to Her Job Rights*. Washington, D.C.: 1974.

Women's Rights Almanac, 1974. Bethesda, Md.: Elizabeth Cady Stanton Publishing Co., 1974.

INDEX

225